AF587347

THEMATIC GUIDE

THROUGH THE MUSIC OF

PARSIFAL

WITH A PREFACE UPON THE LEGENDARY MATERIAL OF THE WAGNERIAN DRAMA

BY

HANS VON WOLZOGEN
BAYREUTH

TRANSLATED BY E. C. CARRICK

3 EDITION

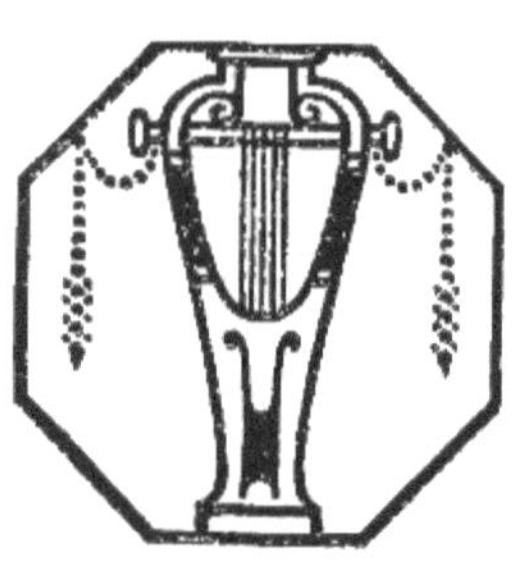

LEIPZIG / GEORG ESSEGER

A Preface upon the Subject Matter of the Music Drama "Parsifal".

Because the dramas of Richard Wagner dealt with early Germanic or mediaeval legends, critics generally have committed the mistake of judging them according to the standard of the existing old German poems upon which these legends were founded. For "Tristan", they have cited the Epic of Gottfried von Strassburg; for the "Ring of the Nibelungen", the Nibelungenlieder. Those, who perceived that Wagner's Nibelungen poetry had little in common with the Nibelungenlieder brought forward instead, the Edda-Lieder, and treated the new drama as a dramatized form of these old Skaldic poems; thus our poet has been reproached for leaving German soil in order to bring his subject matter from a foreign land.

This is incorrect and very foolish. Wagner's subject matter is much older than these confused, fragmentary, Skaldic settings of old beliefs and legendary recollections; not to speak of the epic arrangements of the 13th century. Their characteristic features were first brought to Europe by Aryan races from Asia, and since then with constant changes and condensations have passed into the possession of the Germanic races, especially the German people.

The Eddalieder, in so far as they treat of the Siegfried legend, are German, but outside of this they are Celtic-French, as are also Tristan and Parsifal, whose hidden subject matter, so universally human, was first brought to its full ethical realization by German poetry, and thus became the possession of the German people. But the legendary lore distributed among the nations of Western-Europe was originally in possession of the Aryan-Germanic tribes; and every German poet who has since then seized upon this subject matter and treated it as if it were the original poetical outpourings of our own peculiar national feelings, only made it more than ever our own. When his efforts were in any marked degree successful, he had provided us with what was not only a new, and in itself perfect form of the old matter, but at the same time with an enlargement and explanation of its original, spiritual and moral contents. Both were dependent on the poet's own idiosyncrasies and particular school of art, and these again were determined by the times in which he wrote. The singers of the middle ages created epics expressing only the spirit of those ages, and it never occurred to the poets of later times to present these same works, perfect in their own style, in a modified form as expressing the spirit of another age. Therefore it was folly to suppose that by simply taking the leading characteristics of the epic and putting them in dramatic form that one would create a real Tristan or Nibelungen drama which would satisfy the demands of a modern world. Well might the public assume an unsympathetic attitude towards such a piece of literary trickery.

We can not arrive at a perfect realization of the old subject matter by an outward change of form, nor by a mere sketch of the contents even when put into the best poetical setting. "Daily" it must be „conquered" anew; and such a conquest Wagner made when he adapted this old material to the new musical drama and made it appeal to the sympathy of a generation elevated and refined by works of art. It was necessary to bring out the fundamental and universally human element contained in this much changed and ever altering legendary world. But then, it had to be worked out and put into a form suited to the knowledge and view of the world of the national spirit which had in the meantime developed — a form, engendered by this same spirit, which was destined to furnish him with a pure and "stylvollen" mode of expression.

Inspired by such a desire the Singer of the "Niebelungenlied" wrote in an entirely new form according to the "epos" of that time the old legendary material with the power and individuality of the at that time Christian German spirit. The more the national spirit outgrew its historical garments the nearer it approached the universally human element in the material and thereby arrived at art in its purest form; what exists today in this national spirit, first as purely German, then as that deeply rooted, sympathetic, life consciousness common to humanity, and lastly as a' tendency to artistic ideatity, was concentrated in the personality of a tragic poet, the breath of whose creations was music; and this personality embodied the developed national spirit in a corresponding but new form of the old material.

Because music the most highly developed artistic mode of expressing the true German spirit was given him as his mother tongue, Wagner was able, even in these modern days, to reanimate the old material; this we perceive at every good performance of his works. The high ideality of the subject allowed him to take as the basis of his creative fancy, not only the heathen mythology — to which it originally belonged, — that is to say, those heroic pictures as portrayed in the national poetry of old Germany — but also the realm of the highest Christian ideality as symbolized in the Grail. But had we not music from Bach to Beethoven this ideal would have remained unknown to us, as it remained partly unknown to those singers of the Nibelungenlied who had only words at their command. German music in its sphere has realized for us that for off ideal, and made it a familiar sublime reality. In the musical drama the gods and goddesses of those ancient days an endowed with life as being splendidly typical of those passions and thoughts which are in reality the fundamental supports of all poetic material; and the heavenly, for off sublimity of the God created Christ man as portrayed in the legend of the Grail (since the time of Wolfram von Eschenbach inseperable from the subject matter of Parsifal) becomes also a reality.

Wolfram was not the first writer who infused the religious spirit into the legend, — the combination of the heroic Parsifal with the religious Grail-Saga already existed and had been achieved in the poems of Chretiens de Troyes —; but in Wolfram the spirit of the Grail legend pervades the whole poem with so much sacredness that we here first recognize the full significance of the combination.

But we can by no means take Wolfram as a standard for all time, his writings bear throughout the mark of their own day: his Grail chivalry is the "ecclesia militans" glowing with all the splendor of the chivalry of the Middle ages, his Christian spirit is the spirit of the church of his day, even although the poet displayed it with so much individual force. A writer after the time of Wolfram would not dare to seperate Parsifal from the Grail, he would also need to portray in the Grail the essence of deepest religion as it is understood by a true Christian soul of our own day, who has by spiritual strength arrived at an advanced stage of religious development. Whatever was of value to the new musical drama in the religious ideal found in Wolfram's poems, or in any other settings of the old substance, Wagner added to the structure of his religious tragedy, now perfectly created and called a Sacred Drama.

The seperate parts of the legend we shall now shortly consider, especially as they form the leading characteristics of the music drama with which this work has to do.

The Grail

refers to that holy vessel spoken of in the oldest legends of the Aryan people wherein was contained the divine drink, that intoxicating result of ancient culture, that spiritualized product of nature. They believed that by partaking of Soma, Hoama, Wine, Mead they received the spirit of God. Inward elevation, purification, and strength to serve their God bound the partakers together in a mysterious holy brotherhood: especially so in Eleusis, where Demeter and Dionysos were partaken of in bread and wine. This is the prototype of the Christian sacrament. The Celts in the British Isles also ascribed a holy vessel to Ceridwen, their Ceres, or Demeter. In a later legend after the Christian era it appears as a charger in which lies a bloody head. The blood of their God, (like the torn body of Dionysos Zagreus among the Greeks,) assumed here in the North a material shape for which the legend of John the Baptist may have served as a model. This legend, (given by the so called Mabinogi MS. of the 14th century) is that of Peredur, which corresponds exactly with the story of the French Perceval. No matter whether the origin be Celtic or French, at any rate we first find in France the appelation "Grail" and the story that this was the holy vessel used at the Last Supper. This holy vessel (with the the Patena) was given by the Saviour to Joseph of Arimathea — who caught therein the blood of the Crucified One — that it might preserve his life in prison till Titus released him, and was baptised by him. In Titus we find the first traces of the Titurel who afterwards appears in the Grail. We hear of this holy vessel in the "Perceval le Galois" or "Comtes de Graals" of Chretiens of Troyes († 1190) as a holy,purifying heirloom inherited from Joseph by the kindred of Perceval. In the poems of Wolfram who wrote in 1210 in the same style, there suddenly appears, instead of the vessel, a stone which was brought to earth by the heavenly hosts and was in the keeping of the "Templeisen", the holy knighthood of Titurel who lived on Monsalvatsch, a sacred mountain, inaccessable to sinners. Receiving every Good Friday from the consecrated bread given them by the holy dove, new power to work miracles, we find in this knighthood of Wolfram, a manifestation of divine nature, with direct allusion to the Last Supper and death of Christ. Wolfram ascribed the tradition cf the stone to the poet Kiot, on the authority of Telegetanus (which means in Arab. astronomer) a half Jewish Spanish-Arabian, — this points to Oriental astrology. At one time in Spain the Christians under Pelayo fled before the Moors and retreated into the mountains in the North taking with them the sacred relic; undoubtedly this event offered a splendid opportunity for the formation of such a body as the

Grail Knighthood.

These, taking their ideal from a religious knighthood in the Middle ages, represented the ancient mystic brotherhood. We find in these knights, (called Templeisen by Wolfram)

many points of resemblance to the Templars mentioned in the old Gallic legend of "the head in the charger." They were specially represented in Northern Spain as successors of the Gothic opposers of Paganism. The Templeisen were fed and strengthened by the Grail; from afar they heard the cry of suffering and went forth into the world to shield the innocent and punish the guilty. The names of those chosen were inscribed on the Grail. These were the knightly embodiment on earth of divine love. In all their legends we read that they bore besides the Grail, as a symbol of Knighthood,

The Bloody Lance.

Although Mabinogi did not recognize in this, a relic of Christ, Chretiens of Troyes, on the other hand, identifies it with the spear of Longinus which pierced the side of the Holy One. In Wolfram's writings all trace of this signification is lost: the bloody spear which was greeted with loud lamentations by the Knights of the Grail when carried round their hall, was a poisoned weapon with which a Pagan, while struggling to gain possession of the Grail, gave Titurel's successor, Amfortas, King of the Grail, who was engaged in a love intrigue, an incurable wound. This Amfortas is

The Infirm King

who appears in all the legends. Mabinogi represents him as a lame old man, Peredur's uncle; but in this narrative his infirmity has little connection with the story; the lance and bloody head here introduced have reference to the murder of Peredur's father, and the object of the hero's life is to avenge his death. In Chretiens' writings the infirm king (Le roi pecheur) is the king of the Grail; Wolfram mentions the name Amfortas which signifies weak or suffering but also speaks of his white haired grandfather Titurel who was represented as confined to bed in the Grail mountain. The figure of Amfortas represents, in the knighthood, Suffering incurred by sin. The offence was sensuality, a transgression against the laws of the holy order; the spirit of Paganism which is the embodiment of sensuality inflicted the punishment. In both versions salvation is to be brought by a promised knight who will come and "question". This knight is the hero of the united Grail and Persifal legends:

Peredur - Perceval - Parzival - Parsifal.

He is so far the antitype of Lohengrin, for we see in the latter the knight who went forth to save, whereas Parsifal only sought and asked for the Grail — or wandered without asking. The ideal longing to possess the Grail (which must forever be hidden from sinners) is the highest ambition of holy knighthood; it is the ideal striven for in lifes battle, manifested in the death of Christ, represented and partaken of in the Sacrament of Faith. —

The Gallic name Peredur is explained by "Per-gedur" which means "the cup seeker". On French soil the hero is first heard of as "the seeker for the Grail". To derive the name Parzival from the Gallic "Per-kyfaill" was even more harzardous than to explain it, as Görret did, by the Arabian "Parseh-Fal", which means "the pure, simple one" (der reine Thor). As such he was now to be represented in all legends. For by purity and simplicity salvation was to be brought. The stories of the hero's childhood as told by Mabinogi agree with the later representations of Chretiens and Wolfram. Fatherless, he was brought up in solitude by his mother. The ignorant boy was tempted to go forth into the world by a vision of knights; according to Chretiens he went forth in a peasant's dress and according to Wolfram's in a fool's. The latter calls him "der tumbe klare" and also "der reine Thor", son of Gamuret and Herzeloyde a descendant of the house of Anjou. Mabinogi relates that after many foolish adventures he comes to the castle of his lame uncle but did not ask the signification of the bloody lance and the head. According to Chretiens and Wolfram he arrives at the mountain of the Grail where it has already been announced that he by his question will heal the infirmity of the king. But the simple one does not ask the question. Once more he returns to the world in search of knightly adventure. There the curse of this sin of omission overtakes him, according to Mabinogi as a wild dark haired maiden, according to Chretiens as "la demoiselle" according to Wolfram as "Kondrie la sorcière", the witch, also a messenger of the grail. Now he must wander and seek until he finds again that Castle Wonderful. And he meets a holy or repentant knight who in all accounts reproves him for carrying arms on Good Friday. According to Chretiens and Wolfram the hermit knight gave no further information regarding the Grail. Mabinogi makes the entertainer of Peredur a hermit; while Chretiens and Wolfram represent him as a former teacher of knightly virtue, named Gurnemans and also as one who later giver information concerning the Grail (Wolfram's Trevrezent). At last the seeker finds the castle; according to Mabinogi he revenges his father's death, according to Chretiens he mends a broken sword and cures the king by asking for the lance and Grail, according to Wolfram the cure is wrought by asking the question "What ails thee, uncle?" He reigns as king in his stead.

Wagner's Parsifal.

The simple story which Wagner tells contains all the leading characteristics of this legendary material. He is the pure, simple one, the posthumous son of Gamuret and Herzeleide, who tempted by a vision of knights leaves the solitude of the forest and goes forth into the world. By foolishly slaying an animal, he accidentally discovers the kingdom of the Grail. The suffering of king Amfortas is the result of a struggle with Klingsor, the representative of Paganism (this is the famous sorcerer we read of in all German fables) and this also while engaged in a love intrigue. The lance is the sacred spear of Longinus; the king goes forth to battle bearing the holy relic; Kundry who is in the power of Klingsor, clasps him in her arms; Klingsor robs him of the sacred spear and wounds him; only by the touch of the spear can he be healed (Wolfram talks of the wound being "cooled" by the spear). But the spear can only be regained from Klingsor by the "pure, simple one" (der Reine Thor) promised in the writing on the Grail, who will preserve his purity when brought in contact with sin; this can only happen when he has the strength given to him by consciousness of Amfortas' sin, and this consciousness can only be gained by the deepest sympathy with the sufferer. So runs the writing of the Grail:

"Made wise by pity
This fool will be.
Wait for him
Chosen by me."

Thus the epic "question" becomes a dramatic motive. According to Wolfram the question was superfluous because Parzival knew the answer before he asked it but in the epic it represents the pity he felt for the king and thus symbolizes the deed of mercy incumbent on the hero. This deed of mercy according to Wagners is quite dramatic and takes the form of action, namely: he must regain the spear, instead of merely asking a question: he must touch the wound with the spear he has regained, as a healing act of knowledge born of pity. Gurnemanz the armorer of the knighthood (in whose person we find united in the drama both hermit and knight, two distinct charactersin the epic) believes that this simple one who has so miraculously discovered the kingdom of the Grail, is the promised one and leads him to the feast of love in the castle. But although filled with unknown pain — Parsifal fails to understand the suffering of the king. Once more he is cast forth into the world of folly and wickedness and in the magic garden of Klingsor he is brought in contact with sin. But even in the very arms of Kundry he withstands temptation, for now, when tempted himself, he remembers the sufferings of Amfortas and awakes to a full understanding of their sinful significance. Now grown wise by true sympathy he wins the spear from the destroying hand of the mighty sorcerer. But because of Kundry's curse he is compelled to wander for many a long day. With no power save his own he must now guard and preserve the sacred relic, the knowledge of sin and suffering, amidst the dangers and animosities of the world, in many a hard battle; then only will he find again the way to the Grail. On Good Friday he reaches the sacred kingdom, the weapons of worldly warfare must be laid aside on the day of redemption; and with the sacred and now purified spear he heals, in the sanctuary, the sinner's wound. He reigns as king.

Wagner's Grail.

The Grail as also the spear has its full religious significance. Both symbol's are represented as having been brought (like Wolfram's stone) to earth by the heavenly hosts and delivered into the keeping of Titurel who built For them a sanctuary ("which no sinner findeth") on a mountain in the North of Spain that réfuge in ancient days for the pure faith. This account agrees also with that of Albrecht von Scharffenberg (Wolfram's successor) the writer of "jüngeren Titurel" (1270); but while in his writings everything served to epically display the glories of chivalry, in Wagner's narrative there is a deep religious meaning and it is pervaded throughout by the spirit of the Christian Sacrament, the Last Supper and death of Christ. This is portrayed by the participation in the Communion by the pure and holy of the order, whereby after having partaken of the actual blood and body of Christ they are filled with His spirit and go forth to fight in the cause of justice and innocence, showing forth heavenly love by deeds of mercy on earth. Because of Amfortas' sincaused wound, the Holy One himself must suffer and go forth into the world of sin that he may care for sinners. But the Godlike power which springs from knowledge born of pity frees him from the sorrows of human sin and brings "Salvation to the Saviour." Having thus hallowed the legend which refers on the one hand to the oldest significance — mystery — and on the other to the ideal conception which made the Christian hope of salvation a possibility, the dramatic contrast to Christianity (as embodied in the knighthood of the Grail) could only be found in Paganism. This contrast was already shadowed forth but not fully developed, especially in the larger epic poems. The chivalric epics have represented much more the famous knighthood of the Round Table than that of the Grail. In all legendary poems beginning with those of Mabinogi, Parsifal is said to have joined the court of King Arthur. Wolfram made much more of the contrast; at Arthur's court amidst the highest knightly splendor in the world the curse of the messengers of the Grail (Kundry) falls upon him; and when he returns penitent to this same court she tells him that he is free from the curse. This legend of the court of King Arthur, an imaginary picture peculiar to the Middle ages, could not be used in constructing a religious drama in our own days; its whole character is that of the chivalric Epos, which existed (even with Wolfram) on the numerous adventures of Arthur's Knights. Its association with the legends of the Grail and Parsifal was unnatural and merely external, caused by the ever increasing need of the greedy epic for new material. The proper contrast to the Grail is found in the „Chateau merveil" the enchanted palace of the heathen Klingsor, which in Wolfram's narrative forms merely an episode. Wolfram's Master of the Mirror and of the Four hundred Captive Maidens can be identified with

Wagner's Klingsor,

the unknown enemy of the Grail who wounded King Amfortas. Besides Parsifal, who represents earthly chivalry, Wolfram introduces, with Klingsor and his confederate Orgeleuse, Gawan and many names of magic flowers and wreaths, mystically symbolic, which are also to be found in the account of the Grailking's love intrigue. Wagner utilized every thing which might have reference to his hero Parsifal who is even mentioned by Wolfram as a predecessor of Gawan rejecting the love of Orgeleuse. He gave to the pure one, cast forth by sin into the world to wander and seek, a simple and dramatic form which yet coincides in every particular with the descriptions given in all kindred legends. Orgeleuse, the temptress, he identifies with Kundry the messenger of the Grail, who cursed Parsifal, and with the mistress of Klingsor's flower spirits.

Wagner's Kundry.

This is the most interesting of all the character creations the poet undertook for his drama. In this figure are combined nearly all the varied and seperate personifications of the womanly element, which were to be found in the epic settings of these legends. All these women had their origin in one mythical image, namely, in the Germanic Walkure, and further in the many multiplied forms of the mothers and wives of the Gods. Kundry is depicted in all the legends as having this Walkure nature, and therefore she is at one time represented as malevolent, at another helpful, and again saving. Thus she represents the two sides of woman's character as we find it delineated in these fighting, slaying, protecting, beneficent, mythical Walkure. In all the legends she first curses the hero and then removes the curse or helps him by telling him his fault, thus she (as in Mabinogi) appears transformed to a beautiful youth. This two sided character with its mythological foundation Wagner condensed for dramatic purposes; he further identifies her with the Herodias of the German legend. Herodias is also a Walkure figure, a Frau Hero or Herke — an everlastingly restless spirit that wanders to and fro on the earth; and here we find her likeness to Kundry, the wild horse woman of the Grail, whose Northern name, Gundryggia, is to be found every where in the Eddalieder as personifying the Walkure or fighting spirit. It was said that Herodias laughed as she bore the head of John the Baptist in a charger, and the bloody head blowing upon her, she was doomed from that time to wander. So she became a feminine Ahasverus, consort of the wild hunter Hackelberg, which means "mantel bearer", "Wodan asgod of storm and death. In Wagner's narrative this demoniacal partnership is formed between Kundry and the sorcerer Klingsor, the Gallic equivalent to whose name is Gwyddao, Gwodan, Wodan. As in the Gallic legend the bloody head was symbolic of the suffering Saviour himself so Wagner's Kundry laughed not at the bleeding head of John the Baptist but at the cross bearing Christ: she encountered his gaze and was doomed thenceforth to laugh and wander through the world trying to find the Saviour who by love could free her from the curse. She shows her penitence by good deeds, and serves the Grail: but the curse of her sin urges her ever anew to evil. Klingsor the representative of Heathendom and the sworn enemy of Christ who is alone safe from her alluring wiles by reason of his own wicked deeds, has power over her while she is lying in the charmed slumber of weariness. He compels her to serve him by assuming a beautiful form, woman's most dangerous and alluring side, which gives passion power whereby she works destruction to the knights of the Grail. She has corrupted Amfortas; but Parsifal the pure one resists her temptations. Impelled by her hopeless longing for salvation through love, the unhappy one seeks to find this saving, Godlike love, which her fallen nature craves, in the sinful passion awakened by her devilish beauty. Only one, Parsifal, grown wise by true love born of pity understands the mad folly of this course and tears himself from her embraces. She being thus repulsed curses him; but the victory of purity has deprived Klingsor of his power, the spear is now in Parsifal's hand. Freed from her demoniacal master, and humbly penitent, Kundry enters the service of the Grail; after Parsifal returns to the sacred kingdom, the ever langhing one weeps when she receives the blessing of baptism from the hands of the new king. Thus salvationis extended to the sinning woman. Redeemed, and filled with the radiance of God's grace, she dies; but the redeemed knighthood strengthened anew by the light of the revealed Grail, continue to perform deeds of Christ like pity and mercy in the service of the sanctuary of Godly love, now freed from the suffering of sin.

The Object of my Guide.

I have already spoken of the "motive" in a long introduction to my commentary on the "motive" of the "Götterdämmerung" (Mus. Wochenblatt 1877, No 8 and 9), also in the preface to the fourth, enlarged edition of my guide to the "Ring of the Nibelungen", and lastly with the greatest possible brevity in my guide to "Tristan" (Leipsic, Senf) in the chapter on music. I do not wish to repeat here what has been so often said before, but only to remark that it treats of musical themes commonly called "motives" which form the basis of both symphonic and dramatic phrases. On the one side they are worked out according to the external, but still in regard to style, well established laws of symmetry, contrast, change, repetition — on the other, according to the inner laws of the drama, they are interwoven, assimilated and much varied. While their discovery is the marvelous work of genius the true artist appears in their further musical development.. In compositions in the musical dramatic style, the creative power must of necessity be animatedly sustained throughout; it is not sufficient to erect a structure of artistic beauty alone; the music tone should follow the most subtle motions, shades, moods, and feelings of the poem. The development of the themes should be a musical reflection of the dramatic movement; that is to say, it should portray the inner spiritual power of the poetical situations and motives.

To discover how an artist rythmically and musically employs and varies his themes, how he works them out in a new style and adapts them to longer pieces or shorter figures, is very interesting to the musician, without any special reference to the drama as such. I have not written this work for the musicians, they must treat Wagner's compositions from their own special standpoint. I can tell them nothing in their field which they do not already know better than I, and to discourse thus would not assist the unprofessionals; these are in my position, they are not professional musicans. But just for them I have written these guides in order to give them a general idea of Wagner's style of organizing, and of the harmony existing in his works between the musical and the poetic motives. I have heard that many have had to thank a previous acquaintance with my writings for a true enjoyment of Wagner's works. I do not at all claim that my works give enjoyment. Music acts directly on the feelings and no kind of reflection can ever supply the place of this receptive element. But the path to feeling is less free than is commonly supposed. So it sometimes happens that too great ignorance regarding the poetry which gives expression to the music, or prejudice arising from a false conception of the meaning, or musical ideas limited to old forms, hinders and interferes with the direct action of the music. An earnest perusal of these remarks may among other things help to counteract such predispositions; on the other hand I believe that they will serve as a help to a better understanding of the direct action of the artistic object. Even this may be of some use.

One word more! I must adopt my method of giving distinctive names to those themes which I desire to make prominent and impress upon the memory. This is often difficult and can never be wholly successful, since the musical soul of a motive cannot be perfectly grasped. My names are only of value as marks of recognition, others may choose entirely different and better names than I. The baptismal ceremony cannot be dispensed with when we desire to speak of motives which are not confined to any single part of the symphonic movement, and could not therefore be expressed by numbers. This was proved to me by an amusing experience of recent date: even before the publication of the piano arrangement there appeared in the "Berliner Musik Welt" several rather hasty and superficial articles on the subject, and the author of them, for fear he should be thought a seeker of musical guides, addressed a few energetic words of protest against my particular kind of work, and closed in the following remarkable manner:

"If I give names to motives, it is not that I intend to adopt a bad habit, but because I wish to make more prominent and intelligible certain salient points whose meaning is obvious."

Consequently he makes use of the following: the Bell motive, the Swan motive, the Klingsor motive, the Magic motive, the Grail motive, the Spiritual motive, the motive of the Last Supper, the Redemption motive, and the Triolen motive of the flower girls, Parsifal's heroic motive, the Pain motive of Amfortas, the Kundry motive, and the motive of "the wandering Jewess". Accordingly I have thrust myself into the danger of being accused of plagiarism by making use of these designations, and holding fast to my "bad habit" I write in the same "unmannerly" style this my last "thematic guide" — for:

the Music of "Parsifal".

The Overture

leads us to the sanctuary of the Grail. We hear the solemn, earnest melody, sung at the end of the first act during the love feast of the Knights. They are not manifesting to the world, as in Lohengrin, the power of the Grail, by coming forth from a mysterious distance in knightly splendor to render assistance; but the divine power of love and faith which disclosing itself to the human heart can create from believing souls a holy brotherhood fervent in the service of God. The message of everlasting love, which had compassion on mankind and offered itself up a sacrifice for their salvation, sounds tenderly and lovingly through the perfect stillness, with the intoned melody of the "Speech at the feast of love", (Liebesmahlspruch) (I 1.):

I. Der Liebesmahl-Spruch.

1. a. (Schmerzensfigur.)

Nehmet hin meinen Leib, nehmet hin mein Blut,

b. (Speermotiv.)

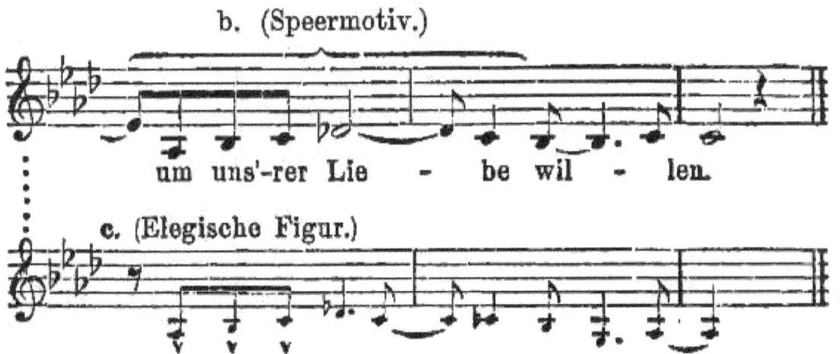

Amidst the soft tremolo harmonies of the string instruments, the divine spirit of love enters the longing and waiting hearts of the worshippers, and as though drawn heavenward by these thrillings of the inmost soul, they repeat the sacred words in gentle prayer. The second part of the speech follows in the same manner (I. 2.):

The brotherhood of faith is now firmly united; and, as though springing from the musical spirit of the speech, the sublime form of the Grail appears with solemn splendor, in the ascending figure of the true Grail motive (II):

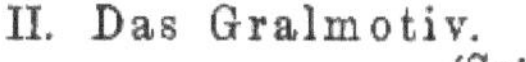
II. Das Gralmotiv.

(Spätere Schlussform.)

Here the music, which hitherto appeared as though softly borne from afar on angels' wings, reaches for the first time, a forte, with which is introduced, triumphant and grand, the third principal motive of the Grail — the "Faith" theme (Glaubensthema) (III):

III. Das Glaubensthema.

2*

that lofty melody sung by the boys at the feast: "Faith lives! the dove doth hover, the Saviour's gracious messenger." Here, introduced by the wind instruments, it resounds as a call of faith to the whole knighthood in the service of holy Love; when the Grail motive has once more gently answered its first appearance (which passes away diminuendo), there begins, starting from *p.*, and gradually increasing to *ff.*, a sublime play of its themes, passing with the different instruments from high to low: a picture of the brotherhood of mankind, which is repeated at the close of the first act, when the knights after the Love feast solemnly embrace one another. Dying away *pp.*, the same theme is once more heard from the heights in this glorious, universal song, as if the blessing of Heaven was being given to the divine union on earth; then it vanishes in a deep roll on the kettle drum, as though a dark curtain of clouds was drawn before this sublime picture of holy bliss. This closes the first part of the overture.

Almost imperceptibly, with low groans, this ominous roll changes from the fundamental tone of the overture ("*a♭*") to a thrilling tremolo on the sixth and tonic ("*f*", *a♭*") and therewith is disclosed the other and worldly side of the Grail, the picture of the sufferings of divine love in the world and in the human heart. With the fall of Amfortas, sin and want have entered the holy sanctury of the Grail. But here in the overture the tones of suffering may be taken in a more general sense. The holy one who gave his body to be crucified as atonement for mankind, dead and suffering in sin, is every day crucified anew in the sinful human heart, and even the holy souls in that faithful community are not free from the curse of an ever renewed desire to sin. Thus the melody of the Liebesmahlspruch is now heard rising from the deep tremolo of the basses, but breaks off almost immediately in its passionately sorrowful middle phrase (I. 1. a) amidst a plaintive tremolo on high notes whose sudden entrance makes it appear as if the whole musical world were rent in twain by the dying agonies of the crucified One. The middle movement is now seperately and sighingly repeated. Twice the melody of the

Liebesmahlspruch passes before us in different keys, in its most sorrowful form, as if in renewed suffering, and the third time having risen with each repetition a minor third higher it appears in the sad key of "*d*" minor; its middle movement is thrice repeated and is taken up by the instruments one after another. It is as if we saw that pierced and bleeding Christ, that supreme passion of pain, that grieving but still silently grieving One; then the closing movement (I. 1. b) joins in, and after being three times interminglingly repeated passes into the simple but impressive Elegiac figure (I. 1. c.). Already the idea of future solace is shadowed forth, and appears as a Chant which afterwards forms a part of the song sung by the youths at the feast. — "The sinful world with a thousand pains etc" (XIV) Now the suffering is past — only a few gentle sighs — the closing portion of the Liebesmahlspruch is heard, then sinks into the depths: and, depicting the blessed trust of the believer in the everlasting love of God, which shall continue when sorrow and death are no more, the first part of the Liebesmahlspruch with the soft tremelo accompaniment (as at the beginning of the overture) soars to the heights, like a ransomed soul to heaven.

The First Act.

The first scene of the first act is divided into two parts, rest and motion — events and narrative characteristically mark the distinction.

I.

The first scene discloses Gurnemanz and the armor bearers silently engaged in their morning devotions; trumpets sound the call to awake, and repeat the Grail motive of the overture. Gurnemanz then calls upon the boys to arise and their quick movements are accompanied by a drastic variation upon the "Faith" theme (Glauensthema III, 1), which like a tuneful spirit can by traced through all the actions of this faithful knighthood; now in an abridged form we hear the principal figure, with a martial and vigorous developement which serves later on to portray the rash and walike desires of Amfortas. Now it seems as if a strong hand is put forth to quell the rising storm: "It is time now to wait on the king" — this is sounded forth on the languid tones of figure (IV), which afterwards in the form of a Suffering motive accompanies the entrance of Amfortas on a litter.

Here we see side by side the splendor and the sorrow of the knighthood; the third element — Hope enters almost immediately in the harmonies of the "Speech of Promise" (Verheissungsspruch) "of the pure, simple one" (V), which are united to in the words of Gurnemanz addressed to the knights who now appear on the scene: "Fool's we, to hope for help from thence" and "only one can help him, only one".

V. Der Verheisungsspruch (Thorenmotiv).

Suddenly a motive belonging to the second part breaks in, preceding the appearence of Kundry; amidst a rushing unison of octaves the Wonder draws near; a stormy movement — one might almost call it martial — springs forth from below and rises chromatically with short vigorous leaps; having reached a fortissimo the true characteristic Kundry motive (VII) rushes downward through four octaves: "There the wild one leaps down"! — What here signifies merely a downward leaping is in reality the musical symbol of Kundry's curse which follows her throughout the whole drama; it is a movement of the most passionate restlessness; thus the demon of her sin pursues the unhappy one from world to world. It also portrays her never ceasing demoniacal laughter, the echo of her curse from her own bosom, so in this wondrous legendary figure we have a perfect musical illustration of the curse, and the accursed.

VI. Kundry's stürmische Figur (»Rittmotiv«).

VII. Kundrymotiv.

Two short chord connections, gently clarified at the word "Balsam" — and when Gurnemanz asks, "from whence hast thou brought this?" a few uniformly descending thirds; this depicts Kundry the "helpful" as we shall again find her in the third act. But at the mention of "Arabia", the home of her magic, the chromatic harmonies of the Magic motive (Zaubermotiv) threaten softly in three long protracted tones (s. IX), which are afterwards constantly associated with "Kundry in Klingsor's service". So the image of this strange woman passes fleetingly but still characteristically before us.

Again the "Suffering motive" (Leidensmotiv) of Amfortas rises before us, with its impressive, chord accompaniment. The sad procession draws near, with the king reclining on his litter, and it is greeted by Gurnemanz with a touching, and plaintive cry. At the words "Lord of a victorious race", a second variation on the "Faith theme" (Glaubensthema) (III. 2.) is introduced.

III. 2.

This strain so full of blissful pride — is a reminiscence of those never to be forgotten days when Titurel reigned, and the pure relic was still unstained by sin. But immediately with the words "to see him thus, the slave of his infirmity" low tones, as if coming from the Liebesmahlspruch, remind us of the king's wounds and of the sufferings of the Holy One. Here there is silence for a short space; the litter is laid down. With Amfortas song ("after nights of pain") there is developed from the "suffering motive" (Leidensmotiv) a charming play of simple intermingling melodies: "morning glory of the woods" which we shall often meet later in the "Murmur of the woods" (das Waldesrauschen) (VIII.).

VIII. Das Waldesrauschen.

We cannot stop to consider here all the details of the following dialogue, e. g., the Grail motive and Klingsor harmonies accompanying the mention of Gawan's departure; but it is worthy of notice that the Word of Promise (Verheissungsspruch) (V) is here used for the first time in its full melody: "grown wise through pity, the pure simple one". It appears repeatedly throughout the scene, and indeed throughout the whole act, as a kind of refrain at the end of each seperate part. It now follows the entrance of the Grail messenger (Kundry) into the dialogue, as it did above on the occasion of Kundry's first conversation with Gurnemanz, but with her fierce motive she breaks of further converse, and the king's procession moves on once more towards the lake, while the "Leidensmotiv" sinks down and passes into the "Waldesmelodie". Solitary and silent Kundry and Gurnemanz remain behind in the peaceful glade.

II.

The second part may be accounted epic, but observe that here we do not treat of narrative alone. Gurnemanz' first three movements contain many short answers, which he returns to the impetuous questions of the youths, (who have drawn near) in reference to Kundry, and, without relapsing into a pure narrative tone they lead us to a better understanding of that wondrous and ever present personality in her three fold character of Grail messenger — the accursed one — and the slave of Klingsor's magic.

The first lively movement of Gurnemanz, (with which — when Kundry asks "are the animals here not holy" — the Grail motive strangely and mysteriously harmonizes) contains, whenever the name of the tempestuous, restless Grail messenger is mentioned, figures which burst forth chromatically and partake of the character of Kundry's "Riding" (Ritt) motive.

The second movement — an earnest, pensive contemplation of Kundry's strange and wondrous nature — makes allusion to the origin of her curse — "the glance of the Saviour she mocked" — by the introduction of the Liebesmahlspruch, "to atone for the sins of her former life" which passes into the "Kundry's laughing" motive (Lachende Kundrymotiv), and is followed by a repetition of the harmonies of the "Verheissungsspruch" of the "simple one". The accursed woman longs for this meeting with the "simple one" who will save her, and seeks herself by simple deeds to serve the truth. Both movements close with sentences in rhyme whereby Gurnemanz with fatherly, kindly earnestness, brings within his remarks the comprehension of the boys; this speech is heard in the second movement ("she does them good") in a short variation of the "Glaubensthema".

The third movement ("yes — if she remained oft absent from us" —) the picture of Kundry in the service of Klingsor, is slowly wrought out in the chromatically ascending and descending strains of the "Magic" motive, (Zaubermotiv) (IX) whereby a mystic twilight is diffused over the whole scene. Here the movement borders again on the narrative style but, immediately passes away in the personal agitation of Gurnemanz, when he considers the sorrow brought by Klingsor to the knighthood. Thus the Magic motive passes by a rapid crescendo into a forte, out of which the Kundry motive dashes downwards ("Thou there, from whence hast thou roamed?") in a remarkable, chordlike form of the "Zaubermotiv" — "why dost thou not help us then?"

What follows is as a matter of fact a sad monologu carried on by Gurnemanz, who is buried in thoughts of the dreadful event, the wounding of his king: "Oh wounding wondrous, holy spear!" This sad cry is introduced by th middle and concluding parts of the "Liebesmahlsspruch" whic struggles forth full of convulsive pain in a passionat swelling tremolo. (Remark here, that more especially th middle part of the "Spruch", — this plaintive movemen on the minor second (I. 1. a.), so expressive of suffering — portrays the wound of the Saviour, and also the sin cause wound of humanity, but the ascending concluding movemen (I. 1. b.) is used to represent the holy spear which inflicte the wound). The exit of the king is accompanied by martial variation of the "Glaubensthema" (III. 2 + 1.), whic however, diminishing and retarding is lost in the harmonie of the "Zaubermotiv": "a terribly beautiful woman charme him". These devilish strains are rent by the laugh of th "Kundry motive", wrought up to a fortissimo, — "th spear has pierced him" — followed by the "Pain part" o the Liebesmahlsspruch, which, with the elegaic figure of th close (I. 1. c.) and the broken plaintive "Endspruch" accom panies this powerfully dramatic movement. "It is a woun that ne'er will close". After Gurnemanz' conversation witl the messengers in reference to the king's condition, (during which the "Waving of the woods" is heard again) Gurne manz repeats these words like a gentle despairing refrain

After the youths question regarding Klingsor there follows the really great narrative ("Titurel the holy hero", Var. I of the Faith Theme) a piece of music perfect in itself, as artistic as it is effective, delineating chiefly, in a solemn and mysterious manner the descent of the Grail, and the signs of purity — the "Spear, and the Grail" — by means of a new angelic soaring variation of the "Faith Theme" (III. 3. "Before him bends in solemn sacred night), whereat it is joined by the Liebesmahlsspruch, (through which the Grail motive sounds) with a rythmical change of the Middle movement, leading later to the gloomy Good Friday Motive ("There on the cross")

III. 3.

Now the Grail motive arises in all its majesty, depicting the erection of the scantuary for "the holy relics" The sacred ness of the Grail's splendour is here unfolded to us: the motive goes on intensely and inwardly ascending resounding through the more confined ascending and descending movements of the leading (Haupt) motive, typifying the search of the chosen for the Grail "by paths no sinner findeth"

till the majestic words at the close: "the wondrous powe the Grail to strengthen", when it once more appears dim. By way of contrast, the dark element of the heathen sorc makes itself heard in a gloomy tremolo in the Bass. pleasure which he takes in working evil, lying in wait, ready to corrupt, is expressed in the closely related Kl sor motive (X) and Magic motive (IX), in which str from the Flowermaiden scene in the second act intermi Kundry's Laughing motive ("to evil pleasure" etc.) is wanting in this devilish combination of hate, corrup and destruction. The Klingsor motive dies away *pp.*, the Grail motive rises anew: "When Titurel now gives kingdom to his son", but a violent impetuous figure, the martially extended Faith theme leads to Amfortas suff and combines again the close (Schluss) of the narrative the previous memories of Gurnemanz. And although is a reversion of the course of events it dramatically ences the epic character of the situation. The Spear m — for so we must here name the closing movement o Liebesmahlsspruch — falls before the power of the Ku motive, and the Klingsor motive is repeated continu Magic has won the day, the Spear is in Klingsor's posses and his motive continues in the ascendency during whole part.

X. Das Klingsormotiv.

Again there enters, as a closing word to this great narra the short solemn passage from the prayer of Amfo the Suffering figure of the "Liebesmahlsspruch" expresses fervour; mystically floating Grail harmonies cause the " dream face" to rise up before him, that "speaks to tly". At this point the melody of the Liebesmahls- heard in its fullest significance, but sinking anon to a imo introduces the "Verheissungsspruch" of the "pure, one" which here appears in full. This motive brings st scene to a close.

The second scene of the first act shows us Parsifal in ngdom of the Grail, then the panorama and the "feast e".

I.

The boys are repeating softly in quartett the wonderful of the Verheissungsspruch, but before they reach the quivering sound, as of an arrow in its flight, breaks on the music — it is the beginning of the Parsifal (XI) The wildest commotion arises. The "Swan" of Lohengrin, like the rushing of wings wildly ling and fluttering, sends forth from far and near ed terrified cries. Just as the confusion reaches a Parsifal appears with his exulting ery: "Truly I shoot flies, upon the wing!" — and his own original motive s along, for the first time complete, full of heroic re.

XI. Das Parsifalmotiv.

But this jubilant outbreak of youthful arrogance is almost immediately silenced by the beautiful and impressive admonition of Gurnemanz.

The peaceful stillness of the forest filled with the gentle twittering of birds (Forest melody), the joyous flight over the waves of the holy sea (Swan harmonies), the broken, impressive representation of the death of the swan, (ushered in by the elegaic Schluss of the "Liebesmahlsspruch", taken out of the Parsifal motive) — the language of music such as this had the power to work a mighty transformation in the heart of the guileless boy, and intensely agitated he breaks and throws away his bow and arrow. Here his own vigorous motive is heard ending with a cry of divine pity. Pity has entered the heart of the ignorant one, and his motive, which has formerly sprung forth so boldly sounds softly and timidly, as though inquiring, and accompanies in the following dialogue, with gentle awe, the questions and the ever resounding answer "I know not". When he fails to remember the many names by which his mother called him, the Herzeleid motive (XII) sounds very sadly.

XII. Das Herzeleidmotiv.

This first part of the dialogue is brought to a close by a little orchestral movement; the youths return once more to the king's bath, and some reverently carry away the dead swan; here the "Swan motive" forms a plaintive echo to "Suffering melody" of the King's march.

The second part of the dialogue is worked out in an animated manner. Immediately following the dreamy melodious portrayal of his awakened memories in reference to his mother, Parsifal breaks forth with childih glee into his former motive: "In forests and meadows wild we were at home".

This character of a youthful, unfettered, adventurous life is continued throughout the whole dialogue, in which Kundry also takes part, and is augmented by the introduction of Kundry's "Riding" motive, which nevertheless has a likeness to the Parsifal motive — "and once by the edge of the forest some men all glittring did pass". As memories crowd faster in upon them Parsifal and Kundry take the words each from the other, and the "Riding" and "Parsifal" motives chase one another away in turn. On learning of his mother's death (Herzeleid motive) joy is dispelled; the animation of this movement reaches a climax with Parsifal's passionate attack upon Kundry. The wildness of the Parsifal motive with its cry of pain *ff.* is quickly quenched by the deep long drawn out bass notes of the Herzeleid motive. Kundry hastens to the assistance of the wearied fainting boy and brings him water; it is worthy of notice that the Kundry motive accompanies even this gentle act of the unhappy woman, rising *ff.* from the "Riding" motive. Upon this passionate display of emotion the solemn words of Gurnemanz fall like a gentle blessing: "he banishes evil who returns it with good". From out of the succession of thirds of "Kundry the helper" there comes a melody which is repeated again in the last act, but here it is soon swallowed up in the gloomy Magic motive. And now Kundry begins to stagger, overpowered by magic sleep; her plaintive broken sighs for "rest" are silenced, Klingsor weaves his spells ever more closely around her, until at last she vanishes from sight.

II.

Now for the first time the "Motive of the Bells" (Motiv der Glocken) falls on the ear, and their ever changing chimes are heard through the whole act; during the transition in the rise of the Grail motive, it takes the form of a thematic figure (XIII. 1.) which introduces, in a simple manner, with its characteristic syncopated accompaniment and constantly upward floating harmonies ("a", "c", "e♭"; then "e", "g", "b♭"), the wondrous change from time to space.

XIII. Das Glockenthema.

Therefrom is developed after the inspired strains of the Grail motive — "where is the Grail" — the processional music, which accompanies the moving panorama. Then arise with great power, mournful dissonances ascending and descending as though a wanderer were climbing rugged cliffs, then chromatically descending thirds, their (Wehelauten) "cries of woe, developing into the Lament of the Saviour (XIV), heard later in the song of the youths: — "in the sinful world with a thousand pains (XIV).

XIV. Die Heilandsklage.

It seems as though the strains of the music led us with the worshippers through the realms of the suffering king, as if we really drew near to the hall of the Grail. Twice from the stage the trumpets sound forth the Liebesmahlsspruch, and a constant chiming of bells on the pure motive notes (XIII) proclaim our arrival in the sanctuary which presents itself to us in the magnificently splendid *ff.* of the Grail motive.

The great scene of the Liebesmahl festival which begins here may be divided into five parts, the first of which is composed of three processional choruses, while the second passionately worked out, portrays the preparations for the reveation of the Grail, (Titurel's summons and Amfortas' refusal), in the third the Grail is revealed amidst prayer and blessing, and then immediately closed, in the fourth the Sacrament is solemnly partaken of accompanied again by a triple chorus, the fifth and last comprises the departure of the knights, and the ejection of Parsifal.

The "Bell" motive (XIII. 1.) sounds through the whole the first two choruses, and the manly powerful bass tones of the knights are heard singing in unison as they draw near "for the last time" to the "Liebesmahl". An interlude joining in with the accompanying motive, depicts the more hasty entrance of the boys to the middle gallery. After the Grail motive majestically ascending to a *ff.* at the closing words of the men's chorus has died away amidst the chiming of bells, and all the knights have assembled in the hall, the youths begin their wonderful alto and tenor song, a masterly work of a religious character for three and four parts, with long drawn plaintive sighs which spring from the

3*

Wehelaute of Amfortas, and are intensely expressive of human suffering, rising like the lament of the "redeeming hero" in a "sinning world" (XIV). The interlude of the "Heilandsklage" which is henceforth thematically related to the ascending syncopated chords of the "Bell" motive, — depicts the ascent of the boys to the highest invisible dome gallery, from which descends, without accompaniment, at the end of the youth's song, as if sung by angels, the softly floating "Glaubensthema" (III) — "faith lives, the dove soars" — which begins and is worked out in four voices. The soft fluttering of wings is heard as the Holy Ghost passes through the sacred space; a short refrain *pp.*, four bars from the "Glaubensmotive" and Grail motive, with the low chiming of bells, then perfect stillness reigns: — in awed excitement we await the beginning of the divine miracle.

From the depths of the background, as from a grave the sad cry of Titurel resounds, like the voice of the undying conscience of mankind — "my son, Amfortas, dost thou officiate?" The melody of the words — "must I die, unaided?" — returns again thematically employed with short vigorous syncopations when Amfortas answers — "my father will'st thou officiate?" — and also at his great outburst of despair which follows (wildly entering with the "Kundry motive") — "no! let it remain unrevealed!"

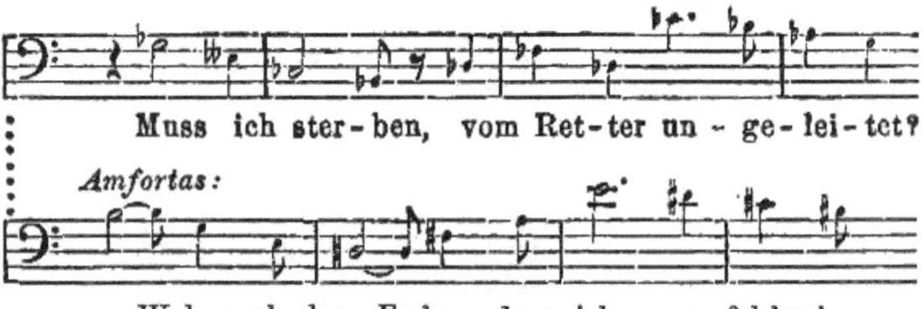

This outburst of despair brings home to our hearts, in a grand tone picture, the sufferings of the unhappy guardian of the Grail. Here the Grail melodies are torn with a perfect passion of pain. "Oh! punishment — punishment unparallelled!" — this heart rending plaintive cry peals forth to the sorrowful strains of the "Heilandsklage" (XIV). And thereafter amidst brightening Grail harmonies, the first passion of emotion gradually subsides — "longingly I must seek him and for his sacred greeting". So yearning the song passes into the Grail motive in soulfully sustained tones; and the "Heilandsklage" dying away *pp.* takes the same upward path of prayer — "I must reach to him!" — where now is revealed gleaming, the vision of the sacred relic, and the whispered words of the royal penitent are softly veiled by the mysterious, upward rising strains of the "Liebesmahlsspruch". — But the sad "Liedensmotiv" of the king (IV) breaks in on the sacred stillness, and sets free the rising and falling waves of the "Zaubermotiv" which rush wildly downaward into the Kundry motive — „in the world of sinful longing with wild fear". From the wound of Amfortas who, captivated by pleasure fell into sin — "wounded by a stroke from the same spear that wounded the Saviour" — pours forth warm sinful blood, as from the pierced side of the Holy One flowed blood drops of pity for sinful humanity. Here the cry of the suffering Saviour issues forth from the plaintive, repeated "Schmerzens-figur" (I. 1. a.). But the Grail motive struggling to ascend is forced to yield to the Klingsor motive which now makes itself heard full of devilish pride trying to excite the hot blood of sin, and the Kundry motive again set free forms a mocking accompaniment to the dreadful despairing cries of the sinner who is longing and seeking for salvation. As at the end of the overture there sounds forth at the last words of his fervent prayer — "mercy! all pitiful One! ah, have mercy!" the expressive, plaintive, elegaic development of the "Liebesmahlsspruch", which then softly dies away amidst the echoes of Amfortas sighs breathed forth with the faint, pleading words — "take my heritage — close my wound." Once more the rising waves of passion are stilled and from above as if touched by an angels hand there falls on the bent head of him who is silently kneeling, the gentle voices of the boys, sending forth the solemn greeting of peace — "grown wise by pity the simple one, wait patiently for him I have chosen". Warningly the deep voices of the knights are heard as they join in a low hushed song. And this part closes as it began with the call of Titurel (terminating in the fundamental tone) — "reveal the Grail".

But the mystery of the scene deepens: amid the sighing strains of the "Liebesmahlmotiv", Amfortas arises, and it rings out ever more clearly from a deep tremolo, in separate fervent parts while the holy cup is being revealed. But deep twilight has fallen and there sounds forth from the highest part of the dome the words — "take my body, take my blood" — accompanied by the soft rhythmless motions of the orchestra and sung by the boys voices in two parts each of them being followed, as in the overture, by the gentle swelling strains of the orchestra. Thus the sacred melody is borne to the heart of the praying king and to the souls of the faithful assembled there together. So divine holiness sheds its eternal light on the earth, and on the most sacred places and depths of the human soul but it lies with mysterious sadness on this lofty Godlike mystery then — as at the end of the overture — the low "After music" of the sacred melody takes up the "Wehelaute" of Amfortas. But at the moment when the son has forgotten his sorrows and is gazing at the Grail which illumines the darkness with its wondrous light — the father's voice arises from the grave in holy rapture — "Oh! sacred joy! how gladly the Lord greets us today".

Soon the soft "after music" of the "Glockenmotiv" passes into the legendary, gently swaying melody of the boy's chorus — "wine and bread of the Last Supper" — which is sung while the knights partake of the Communion. The Youths' voices take up the melody in lower tones. The choruses combine together and almost immediately the double chorus of the knights joins in with heroic strength — "take of the bread, take of the wine". At the first verse the "Glockenmotiv" is heard, at the second, mighty strains like the warcry to a holy battle. Finally the songs of praise sung by the knights', the youths, and the boys intermingle until they form one united soaring strain from the Grail motive, which bears the voices of the chorus, sinking to earth, up to the kingdom of divine love. As in the overture, with the closing development of the Faith theme, the invoked spirit of love comes down into their midst and blesses the brotherhood, who embrace one another.

But the suffering cries of Amfortas break in on the blessedness of the brotherhood; the wound bleeds anew and the king is carried away on his litter. The knights depart, as at the beginning, to the chiming of bells, and the repeated strains of the "Heilandsklage". The theme of the "Pure, simple one" also enters here but Parsifal remains unmoved by the call. When the chiming of the bells has quite died away Gurnemanz turns to him and with short, broken, angry tones from the "Thorenverheissung" asks — "dost thou know what thou hast seen?" But the short figure from the "Liebesmahlsspruch", (I. 1. c.) (expressing such intense pain and longing, and which in the king's cry had so deeply moved him although he did not understand the reason), answers instead of the silent boy. To a violent, ascending figuration of the Parsifal motive Gurnemanz thrusts him from the temple and in the short rhyming words of the Knight the "Song of the Swan" is heard; the exit of the sorely disappointed old man shaking his head and shrugging his shoulders is again accompanied by the short broken form of the "Verheissung". But like a heavenly comforting sign of its unfulfilled oracle the whole Promise ("grown wise through pity" etc.) is heard sung by a single alto voice, and dying away in the heights is taken up by the soaring melody of the chorus: — "blessed in faith". — Then a few deep bell tones and the curtain falls.

The Second Act.

The Overture.

After having been transported to Heaven at the end of the first act, the beginning of the second casts us down to the depths of Hell, form which seems to break loose unrestrained (in the wild "Vorspiel") all the devilish rage of sin and destruction. First the Klingsor motive (XI) arises from the depths of the bass in its most fiendish form and at last reaching a *ff.* in the high positions it remains in the ascendency during the whole of the first half of this indescribably overpowering piece of music. And this fierce exciting beginning leads to the loud, piteous "Wehelauten" of Amfortas (XIV) sounding here like the agonized shrieks of human souls enslaved by evil. Twice they ring out *ff.* in the heights and then wail in the distance, and the Kundry motive ever higher and more shrilly laughing springs forth, repeating seven times in succession, its despairing, hellish cries of triumph. During this second half the Klingsor motiv maintains its power below, at least in its masterly closing notes, which now arise as if invoked and immediately join in the "Magic" movements, here worked out as motives. After the Sorrow chord has been struck for the third and last time in the middle of the Kundry motive, this motive appears for the fifteenth time and now alone, rushes downward through three octaves: the curtain rises, and we find ourselves in the sorceror's tower and he himself ready to summon the unhappy woman to his service to work the destruction of the holy and guileless youth.

I.

In the short scene between Klingsor and Kundry, we see the powers of evil concentrated in the devilish might of the sorceror The motive, which at the beginning creeps along like a snake lurking in the abyss, coiling itself round the "the master of sin" — the "Magic" motive with the "Klingsor" motive predominate through this scene, and show by their combination with the seldom silent Kundry motive the power which evil gains over the unhappy woman. But in between these three ruling motives the speech of the "Simple-"Youth" who is drawing near is heard, with at times a slight reference to the Parsifal motive at the words — "already my magic castle waits for the fool" — and afterwards — "the greatest danger must today be faced" — and again in short measures at the words — "Ha! who withstands three sets thee free" — and also at the end of the scene — "thou childish stripling" etc. But the "Wehelaute" — these thirds so expressive of woe — which until now have always been heard in connection with Amfortas now issue forth in the hellish outpourings of the "Magic" harmonies, like cries of pain coming from the demon's victim and in them perhaps the culminating point of this scene is reached, enveloped throughout in devilish wickedness.

Klingsor has subdued Kundry with his own motive ("Arch fiend, Rose of Hell!") and from out of these slow downward shuddering harmonies the plaintive "Wehelaute" is heard. The figure of the accursed one appears with a dreadful shriek that sounds as if it came in terror from one half waked from deep slumber and from it the Kundry motive bursts forth in a wild uprearing figure.

Moaning and sobbing she strives in vain to find words with which to answer the fierce, mocking call of her master; then, when her Magic motive can only by heard in short sighs there springs forth with the fervent words — "Longing, longing!" — the Wehelaute of the "Heilandsklage" but it passes away almost immediately into a figure which, when Klingsor mocked the knighthood, appeared soaring upward in a light bewitching tremolo, but here it springs up, half defiant half longing, in a violent form of the Kundry motive — "there — I served."

This upward leap closely connected with the "Kundry" motive accompanies, with a laughing echo, the whole dialogue so strangely drastic, violent short, and full of strife — "I will not" — an anguished reminiscence of the elegiac figure (I. 1. c) — "thou must" — "thou canst not hold me" — "but bind thee" — "thou?" — "thy master" — "by what power?" — and so on to the dreadful climax — "Ha! Ha! art thou virtuous?" — when there is a pause in this stormy troubled scene of devilish passion: a pause but no repose, for Klingsor's fury and passion return raging to his own sinful bosom and in that dreadful solitude filled with fearful memories they rend one another. The Klingsor motive lends its tones to these words of the sorceror — „dreadful power of hellish impulse." But here in contrast to the suffering Klingsor the picture of the suffering Amfortas appears as if offering the sorceror malicious comfort; the "Wehelaute" and the "Leidensmotiv" (IV), and ultimately both together, appear after a dissonant shrilly broken of uprising of the Grail motive — "soon I feel that I myself shall be the guardian of the Grail!"

Like the lamentable laughing of a soul inwardly suffering and conquered by the magic power of sin, shrill, devilish chord triplets are heard resounding. They begin with the short stormy dialogue and continue throughout Klingsor's madly defiant and ultimately beseeching cries. When Kundry sorrowfully remembers Amfortas' weakness and the weakness of all who have fallen through her, and knowing that a new victim will soon be brought she struggles once more convulsively, and we hear the broken, syncopated "Wehelaut" of Amfortas: — but she struggles in vain against that rising power, her way to salvation by love leads her, because of her curse, through the poisoned paths of enchanted sin: — "only he who withstands her, can set her free!" — Here *p.* the Parsifal motive sounds. Klingsor moves to the battlements of the tower to follow the movements of the foolhardy boy as he presses onwards; his struggles, his mastery of the knights, his arrival at the magic garden. He watches the scene with Satanic mockery, sure of conquest, and recounts it to the mourning Kundry, while she ceasing to wail, breaks into a wierd laugh and vanishes.

The attack on the castle during the time Klingsor stands

watching is a piece of music full of fiery life; like spring breezes it passes fresh through the magic sphere, and deals blows around with the irresistible, foolish courage of a gay youthful spirit.

Amidst the rushing of octaves, rising ever anew from below, a variation of the Stormy figure of the "Ritt" motive (a) introduces, as if it were thrust upward by the trills of the Kundry laugh, a glorious triumph-song in the complete melody of the Parsifal motive, with the words — „they falter, they fly". But to this is joined a short intermediate movement — "every one bears home ward his wounds" — in which the quick beats of the "Thorenmotive" are again heard, till at last the Parsifal motive breaks in triumphantly, but is muffled in its joyous ascent by a quick tremolo, with which it starts anew stretching itself gently out as if looking around in surprise, and then in a charming figure of the Flower voices it sinks back again into the whirring harmonies of the Kundry Laugh. This is the accompaniment to Klingsor's captivating song melody — "Ah! how proudly he stands on the battlement, how laugh the roses in his cheeks, how childishly astonished he gazes into the lonely gaıden" — but Kundry is already at work and the charm is well and rightly chosen whereby this fool is also to be ensuared, his mother's motive (XII) here joins in softly and while giving him her dying greeting the temptress seeks to seal his soul with the hellish stamp of her kisses. With a crashing *ff.* sinking again to the depths dimuendo the Klingsor motive is heard as at the beginning of the overture, the tower of the sorceror falls, and the magic garden arises before us in all its oriental, supernatural, magic splendor of flowers, these most luxuriantly beautiful productions of Hell's glowing warmth.

II.

During the following scene between Parsifal and the Witch maidens when sweetest melodies pour forth in inexhaustible profusion, the oft repeated Parsifal motive marks off the seperate divisions.

The Parsifal motive begins the first movement, and with a new remodelled form of the Stormy figure, in the style of the previous „Sturmmotiv" (see above b.), depicts in an animated manner the thronging togethor of the terrified girls. Two terzetts for solo voices and two three voiced choirs appear on the scene becoming by degrees more and more vehement. During the vigorous ascent of the repeated, expressive, halftones at the end of the figure the first theme of the Maidens bursts forth in *f*. (XV. 1.): in the accompaniment it whirls along skipping and fluttering with excited triplets midway, continually pressing upward like the rushing together of anxious seekers, while the foundation of the whole — the song of the solo voices — changes about with it, as if the tones also were anxiously and chromatically following: — "my lover wounded!" — — "where shall I find mine?" — and so on.

XV. 1.

This is the Maidens Lament which later on having arrived at a deeper significance and power serves to express the longings for salvation of all who live in this enchanted world. At the climax of the general excitement where the whole chorus joins in the calling and questioning — "where is the enemy?" — and when in the meantime the theme of the solo singers has ascended from "e♭" to "b♭" at the last "Wehe!", a second theme enters (XV. 2.). The maidens have caught sight of Parsifal — "there he stands" — the solo voices cry with terror, the chorus repeats the words, and immediately takes up an accompanying figure which ascends in thirds — "see him there, see him there!" This figure is woven into the instrumental accompaniment of the new theme, which on its side expresses artless surprise in a charmingly mischievous manner, but here because of the general excitement, it portrays terror.

XV. 2.

This theme also ascends steadily and quickly till the first theme once more enters — "Woe! woe! he slew our lovers" — and so on. This also reaches a climax at the repeated, triplets of the "Halbtonschluss" the general outcry ending suddenly in "e♭" — "accursed shallt thou be", — whereupon the Parsifal motive joins in powerfully in a new key.

The Parsifal motive in its perfect development depicts the leap of the youth from the heights, and his first artless laughing words: "Beautiful children! ought I not to have slain them?" are accompanied by the soft extension of the motive, as was the case when Klingsor watched from the tower. And now in a changed tone *p.* the maidens converse with him quietly and kindly; their terror and excitement past, they are inclined to be gay and their conversation is accompanied by the second Theme, so well suited to express Parsifal's mischivous wondering manner. The marvellously tender extension of this theme accompanies the first solo questions and Parsifal's answer. The first theme appears in the little movement "So thou wilt not harm us". At the closing repetition of the Schlussfigur the whole chorus joins in: "Who will play with us now" and a general laughing and running follows Parsifals ready pleasant answer.

Amidst many alluring trills the Parsifal motive is developed into a long interlude.

Wreathed with tender flower melodies this same interlude appears once more, as if developed from a sweet subdued interweaving of the Motivansatz. Here the maidens who have remained in the background also advance toward the now trusted stranger and the others withdraw to deck themselves in secret with flowers. All this takes place lightly and laughingly like child's play, without the intended character of sensuality. This is the sweetness of nature which with playful intoxicating power exercises the spell of wonder over the simple captive. With the words "we do not play for gold" the maidens take up the mischiveous second theme which ascends in a series of trills; now the others having decked themselves with flowers return, and a short contest ensues, accompanied by the gradually descending figurations of the till now triplet themes, which softly abating pass into a lulling peaceful motion. In this manner they float into the (in$^3/_4$ tempo) melody of the long drawn out "Carressingsong" Kosegesang (XV. 3.): "Come, come, gentle youth!"

XV. 3. (Kosemelodie.)

Komm', komm', hol - der Kna - be!

blühen! Komm'! Dir zu Wonn' und
La - be gilt mein min-ni - ges Mühen!
Komm', hol - -
XV. 4.
Schmeichelfigur.)
des Gar - -
3

While the chorus work out the melody, the solo voices enter in a longing caressing figur afterwards characteristically embellished by triplets of semiquavers; "Come, come, oh gentle boy". The solo voices of the second half of the maidens join in, and both choruses combine in the working out of the fundamental melody in which at last all the voices ascend together. "To make thee joyous and happy our loving care we give". The "Schmeichel figure" (XV. 4.) weaves its fragrance closely a round Parsifal's simple nature. "How sweetly you smell! are you then flowers?" — This figure also forms the varied fundamental theme of the following charming song: "Pride of the garden and fragrant spirits" for solo voices, with which the Kosemelodie intermingles in the form of an accompaniment: Finally the chorus joins in softly: "Grudge not the flowers their reward", also at the wonderfully expressive closing words of the solists: "There we droop and die". Here the Schmeichel figure, moving like flower leaves gently stirred by the soft breath of summer, after a few strains of the Maiden's Lament, breaks out cres in tender trills and passes into the returning fundamental melody of the "Kosegesang".

To this second song, which touchingly expresses the longing of the flowers for salvation there is added the coaxing entreaties of the maidens that their gentle comrade will play with them, and they cling round him childishly and carressingly: "Oh take me to thy bosom!" etc. Here the strains of their first song.

Here Parsifal's Call is again heard and also the Parsifal motive softly and in minor, as if in timid defence: "If you will that I play press not so closely around", these words, their now impatient playfellow sings to the strains of the Maiden's Complaint. Here a third — or taken with both of the other songs — a fifth and last theme of the maidens enters (XV. 5.), as if developed from the repetition of the Parsifal motive, chord like, skipping, ascending and descending like merry, lightfooted spirits running hither and thither and constantly interrupted by little warding off movements in the bass at the hurried cries: "Why dost thou scold?" "Because you quarrel" — "we quarrel only because of thee" —

XV. 5.

When the chorus joins in, the element of excitement, heard in the first theme is once more perceptible and the second theme is heard giving a light charming merry character to the song: "See the flowers woo the butterfly." While the maidens are singing all together ("No! he is mine — no ours — yes mine") the last theme brings this play, full of fragrance, and sweet sounds to a sudden end with the Parsifal motive — (in a♭ as at the beginning) "Cease! you cannot catch me!" — which in its turn sinks almost immediately into the wondrous Thorenharmonien: "Parsifal! — wait!" — This is Kundry's first call —

For a short time the "Thorenharmonien" remain floating over the astonished youth; then comes the Herzeleide motive (XII.) "Wait here Parsifal! Greeted thou art by joy and salvation!" The unseen one addresses the maidens, and her sweet voice gently bids them go and tend to their wounded knights; here as they are being sent away we hear their Pleading melody, (XV. I) and also when they gently, plaintively and poutingly one by one leave off playing "To leave thee, to fly from thee!" The whole chorus then joins with the last

Theme, in cres, ("Fare well, thou proud one, thou gracious one") and with the mischiveous spring over the "fermate" (Thou fool) they, softly laughing disappear in the direction of the castle.

III.

In this act the great scene, between Kundry and Parsifal may be devided materially into two parts; the first, and distinctly smaller one, shows how the youth is spellbound by the sweet but painful memories of his mother's forgotten love which are called up by Kundry's exquisitely tender song. The second, on the other hand shows us the moment of transformation with powerful, dramatic intensity, which in spite cf its lengthy development is still concentrated, the awakening of Parsifal to a moral consciousness of his human power to save, Kundry's strivings after salvation by love, and the victory of purity with knowledge, over the infatuated longing of the sinful woman.

As in the former scene the first conversation between the "nameless one" and Kundry the "name proclaimer" takes place amidst the Thorenharmonies; and after Kundry has given her short account of the father's death, the Herzeleid motive enters, in the form of a long drawn out solo song, which is immediately joined by a gentle little figure — a forecast of Kundry's Sacrifice ("Hingebung") melody, which appears later: (s. XIX.) "Here I have waited to tell thee this". These first lines in the picture of love seem as if drawn by the hand of a spirit in the heart of the listening boy, to whom its double, secret nature will soon be revealed.

The first part is almost entirely taken up by the long account which Kundry gives Parsifal of his mother — magic strains from the "far off home" of the narrator lead into the tender love sphere of the Slumber song: "I saw the child on his mother's breast." This sweet lulling melody, already suggested, breathes throughout in a childlike form the spirit of the Herzeleid motive, so that here we have the Idyll and the Elegy marvellously combined. The Herzeleidmotive itself enters when the meaning of the name is indicated: "sorrow in the heart", and at the words "the delight of her eyes rejoiced in her suffering" the motive throws off its elegaic character and takes the lively $^9/_8$ Figuration (compare XII. I.) with which the song is brought to a melodious close. — The second part is worked out in the same style from the same motives: "On the moss twas softly bedded" as far as: "the hot dew of a mothers tears" etc. . . .

XII. 1.

(Leidenschaftliche Figuration des Herzeleide-Motives.)

Here follows an interlude far "from warfare" which is characterised by a low, as if distant martial motive punctuated by $^3/_4$ notes in the Bass, with a regular whirring $^9/_8$ tremolo from which emerges "only sorrow had she" the development of the previous Passionate figure (XII. 1.) with its wild impetuous ascent: "Cannst thou not hear her pleading cry?" then with fierce passion "when she seeking then overtook thee" till the joyful climax: "wildly her arms were cast around thee" when it suddenly becomes dim ($^3/_4$): "Wert thou distressed when thou wert kissed" and then ceases —. Here the second Herzeleide motive appears, intensely sorrowful, as though sighing sadly, in the sorrow of painful memo ries: (XVI).

XVI. Das zweite Herzeleide-Motiv.

Here are portrayed the sorrows and cares of love; first a mother lamenting for her child, then a child for its mother; a small triplet figure joins *sf.* thematically inbetween, expressing inward terror. So the song continues till it reaches with the first Herzeleid motive, its simple, sad, quiet end: "And — Herzeleid — died!" —

Parsifal's piercing cry rings forth from short, monotonously trembling syncopated cres. chords; the expressive figure of the Liebesweh (XVI) accompanies his lament and its deeply sorrowful strains are heard at the words "Gentle mother — forgetting thee". When Kundry sweetly and caressingly comforts him ("Was pain till now unknown to thee") the only answer she receives from the grief stricken boy is a dreary repetition of that tender woeful cry. "Mother — could I forget thee!" — Then suddenly in the Spear motive from the Liebesmahlspruch there arises before him the picture of the sacred spear and the forgotten sufferings of the holy brotherhood: "Ha! what have I forgotten!" Here the Kundry motive burst forth for the first time, and with a quick movement "the Rose of Hell" turns the thorns of that inward sorrow, which springs from the delights of love, to the heart of the sorrow bound youth. This she effects amidst the alluring strains of the Kundry magic motive, (Learn to know that love by which Gamuret was held") and when it ceases there appears the Passionate figure of the first Herzeleidmotive which again ascends to the Kundry motive. Amidst these enchanting strains, strangely and expressively worked out *pp.* by the violincellos she presses on the youth's mouth "the first kiss of love". — The last tones of the chromatic motive, sounding like broken distressed sighs, suddenly draw together, symbolizing new and vigorous but painful life: here the Schmerzenfigure of the Liebesmahlspruch breaks forth from the sighs with sudden strength (as when Gurnemanz told of Amfortas' fall) and draws forth with it *ff.* the "Wehelaute"-Lament of Amfortas. "Amfortas!" — this, Parsifal's second cry of memory — seperates the scene into two parts, and thereafter into the drama of Sin and Trouble, Salvation enters.

The second part of the scene may be devided into three portions: — Parsifal's vision of the suffering Saviour — Kundry's narration of her curse — and the last conversation between these two, culminating in Kundry's outbreak of despair when she curses Parsifal.

The first part of Parsifal's Vision, the loud lammenting cry when Kundry kisses him, and he feels in his own heart the pain of Amfortas' sincaused wound is interwoven with a wild storm of Kundrymotive figures, and Wehelauten: — ("Oh lamentation! Oh! misery!") the piercing tones of the Schmerzensfigur are also heard „I saw the wound bleeding", and it is worthy of notice that at the words: "No, it is not the wound" the Magic motive passes into the Leidensmotiv (IV) then a passage of stormy figures piu *f.* introduces anew the "Wehelaute". "Oh anguish of love" followed by a downward rush of the Kundry motive. This is the climax of the first expression of lamentation — Now follows as contrast the vision of the Grail mystery during which the echoing syncopations of the last wild motive are purified in the majestic harmonies of the Grail: the Liebesmahlthema enters in its mystic might and "every soul thrills with the rapture of redemption". — But the Kundry motive enters once more; the charm is broken and passionate sorrow rends the human heart; the Lament of the Saviour (XIV), (as at the close of the overture) sounds forth in contrast to the rapture of redemption, answering like an echo from the heart of the sinner. Still above all human pain as though rising from the depths of the all merciful heart of God there rings out with convulsive power this plaintive cry "Redeem me, save me from those sin stained hands" to the strains of the Liebesmahlspruch; then ending sorrowfully it dies away in the Schmerzensfigur. With the last fervent words of Parsifal's prayer these woeful echos cease in the sighs of the "Heilandsklage". "How can I a sinner atone for such sin" — a great change has taken place in Kundry's soul: when she now bends low before the "rescued one" (Parsifal) he is no longer to her the victim whom in order to serve Klingsor she must corrupt, but 'the noble knight" the longed for, beloved "Saviour" who by his love can redeem even the goddess of sensuality. This transformation is portrayed by a new motive, a longing, ascending, penetrating figure with an entrancing, heaven ward soaring, beseeching close.

XVII. Das sehnsüchtige Motiv der Kundry.

hold der Huldin Nah'n!

But now in the "Huldin" Parsifal recognises the destroyer of Amfortas, and throughout this second part of the vision, which musically illustrates in detail her alluring caressing beauty, the Kundry motive is constantly heard, and with artistic variatious adapts itself to the finest touches in this picture of temptation (XVII. b.). And when the picture is completed with that "terrible kiss" this motive ascends, and is merged *f.* in the "Wehelaute", but immediately breaks free and flies rapidly upward: "Destroyer! — depart from me" then, as though thrust away it sinks downwards: "Forever — forever — depart from me!"

Immediately Kundry's new Longing motive (XVII. a.) enters with impetuous energy and surrounds, like a love incantation, the first uprising of a melody, already touched upon, which is full of unbounded enthuiastic self aacrifice (s. XIX): "So also feel now" etc. — "Oh couldst thou know the curse", — What but the Kundry motive, the wild musical expression of her curse could here thematically characterise the transition to her narrative? But then — a solemn, anxious pause, and a short gloomy roll from the kettle drums accompanied by a Klagelaute which expresses with its sighing triplet appogiatura the sorrowful spirit of Good Friday: this is a preparation for the vision of the cross bearing Christ.

XVIII. Des Heilands Erscheinung mit dem Charfreitags-Motive.

"I saw Him — Him" — and the Liebesmahlspruch, which softly describes with sublime awe that journey of agony when the Saviour bore his cross, then ends as if wailing in the rythmically broken Schmerzfigur of the Good Friday motive. But the Kundrymotive breaks in hastily and shrilly, ascending exultingly with the wild figure heard before in the Klingsor scene: and "laughs!" — "Then his glance fell on me": and from the long drawn out strains of the "Wehelaute" the ("Heilandsklage") Saviour's Cry arises full of in inexpressible sublime sorrow. Thus the sorrow of God looks down on the sinning world.

But even with the remembrance of divine suffering, magic strains arise, and thrust the Afflicted one forth to the wanderings of her curse; while the Heilandsklage is heard soaring ever higher full of infinite longing. Then it sinks into silence amid echoing syncopated notes; but out of them the "mysterium" of the Grail harmonies arise in wonderful majesty, and form a beginning to the ascent of the sacred motive: the accursed one believes that she will again see her Saviour "Already his glance rests on her" — but the laugh of the Kundry motive breaks in on the blessed sacred peace of the moment, so beautifully expressed by the monotony of the deep tones of the song, and roused to still greater fury by the Klingsor motive in the bass, storms on to the close "Only to scream to rage, to rave, to storm", this is the fate, of the "accursed one". From the depths of her passionate sorrow there arises in plaintive tones of longing a wild demand for that love and salvation, to be found in the arms of the loved hero: "Let me but on his bosom weep, only one hour united be to thee: even if rejected by the world and God, Redeemed and purified by thee I'll be" the entrance here of the Hingebungmelodie lends to these last words an expression of intense enthusiasm (XIX).

XIX. Das hingebende Motiv der Kundry.

Parsifal's Answer: "In eternity thou wouldst be damned with me" is introduced by the same theme as Kundry's former song (XVII): and at the following words "forgetting for one hour my mission" the Thoren motive enters with lofty majesty as a sign of the noble power of healing; but here the Answer takes the form of a passionately expressed warning characteristically distinguishes it from all others both as regards text and music — and appears, to glorify Parsifal's whole personality. Here we see before us the wise "Thor" "the pure one", as a mighty preacher of the true salvation; in accordance therewith, the expression of his song, with it's simple dignified recitative, approaches that elevated declamatory style, (already found in Tannhäuser) in which religious devoutness, as the embodied power of faith, finds "stylvoll" musical utterance. But with the remembrance of the sufferings of the holy knighthood and the necessary atonement, the "Wehelaute" of Amfortas enter, and the passionate Kundry motive is also heard "To mortify the flesh". Here, inbetween, a wonderfully touching song from the "Glaubenstheme" sounds forth: "But who did fully, clearly, see in him, the true fount of salvation?" Indeed this music is of such a strange mysteriously forbodeing character, especially in the voice part, that it could only spring (in this tragedy of a "Saviour's Salvation", from the divine sphere of the Grail itself. The "Wehelaute" and the Kundry motive conclude with Parsifal's last cry lament. — "Oh misery, what a curse". This warning song of the hero, which coming after Kundry's narration of her sorrow appears as if glorified by the sublime vision of the Saviour — and here Parsifal is for the first time the true hero of the Drama. The last powerful climax in this scene is arrived at by a series of lively dialogues, and, especially in the declamation of Kundry's song, with its wide bold intervals ("Attain thou now to godliness" — "consecrate thy time to God") the highest plastic expression of devilish passion is reached. While Kundry in this last outbreak of despairing rage makes use in her song, of the Schmeichelfigur (XV. 4) with protracted intensity, the "Mädchenklage" also joining in later as if fervently invoked, "Let me love thee thou Godlike one" the hero answers her assaults, earnestly and resolutely in a powerful combination of the Parsifal motive with the ascending passage of the Grail motive. Now there remains nothing for the conquered sinner but her own terrible, rushing, laughing Kundrymotive which rages through the whole of her last angry effusion against Amfortas, and is heard even at the words "whom I mocked — mocked" — lending them an expression of unrestrained devilry. The Spear motive is heard full of power through these mocking piercing harmonies, and gives occassion for Parsifal's question: "who dared to wound him with the sacred weapon?" Here the "Stormy figure" springing up, with wild leaps, into a passionate working out of the regulary ascending, chromatic, fundamental form of the "Mädchenklage". "Ha! madness! — pity me!" — closes with a suggestion of the "Hingebungsmelodie"; a burst of longing at the intensely retarded ending: "Mine for reference to one hour — only one hour to be thine!" — chase away the last despairing words, unaccompanied and broken by syncopation —: then comes Parsifal's second repulse, full of horror: "Avaunt! unhappy woman!"

A furious downward spring of the Kundry motive leads to a wild syncopated repetition of the Klagechromatik ("stop his way close his path") followed now on Kundry's side by an angry upward leaping „stormy figur" also heard in the exceedingly characteristic animated song: "and if thou fliest from here, and if thou findest all the paths in the world!" When this figure breaks off above, as if in despairing search for the sacred scantuary "the path to which thou willt not find" — the "Zaubermotiv" arises excitedly from below and Klingsor's motive joins in with threatening growles at the bitterly pronounced curse: "Wander! wander", — here a short Wehelaute "so familiar to me" — and then the wild broken end: "Thou I decree shalt accompany him".

Klingsor himself has appeared on the ramparts and hurls the desecrated weapon at Parsifal; here the Klingsor and Spear motives are heard in combination. But radiant the sun breaks forth from the threatening storm clouds, the splendid triumphant strains of the Grail motive arise, as if carried on heavenly breezes; making the sign of the cross by the power of compassionate knowledge, Parsifal causes "the castle with all its "magic splendour" to fall down in ruins. Like withered flowers the maidens lie on the ground and when the last sounds of the crash have died away in gloomy "tritonus" sounding as if they came from the depths of Hell, the "Mädchenklage" is heard sighing in a tender melody. With Kundry's last glance at the departing figure of Parsifal a lamenting longing cry rises *ff*. full of sorrowful passion. Parsifal turns away and the curtain falls amid the deep tremolo of *b minor* chords.

The third Act.

The Introduction.

with the first tones we enter the melancholy depressing scene of the "Verödung" (XX.) The se tones form the principle theme during the whole of the first half of the act as though they were seeking disappointed, and strains from the music heard later at Titurel's burial, enter during the working out of the theme

XX. Das Thema der Öde.

pp

Trauermusik.

etc.

From this is developed a more animated measure which is however not less sad, hopeless and troubled —: a picture of Parsifal's wanderings. The syncopated, broken variations, of the once stormy Figure of the Rittmotive (VI.) seek anew unavailingly to gain the ascendancy. The chromatically ascending Contrary movement of this motive employed thematically at the beginning of the Overture) can be heard intermingling throughout.

After a short halt on the Verödungstheme, as if it wer casting a desponding glance around, the ascent of th Wandering Theme continues, rythmically altered, with eve greater intensity and vigour, till one almost expects to see i take the form of the Grail motive in its rapid cres Her the motive of Kundry's curse breaks forth with it rapid *ff* and rushing downwards, through three Octaves thrusts th unlucky wanderer away from the sacred goal of his dreams and once more back into the world of trouble and strife.

This is depicted in the following part of the Overture The Speer motive, from the "Liebesmahlspruch", which ros up during the Kundry motive like a holy weapon shieldin from sorrow, and exorting the desponding one to be couragous enters there in combination with the short strokes of th Thorenmotiv. So the guardian of the sacred heirloom must fight in a world hostile to nobility and goodness, against the danger of impurity which ceaselessly threaten him, without allowing th holy weapon to be sullied in the strife. This motive can b heard inbetween, like a battle call, or a longing cry for th expiation of suffering, but is warlike even in it's cry o despair, which rises once more tumultuoulsy to a *ff*.

Here during, a quick transition, the strains of the accompaniement take the form of the Klingsor motive; the Thorenmotive dies away amidst the deep notes of the kettle drums, and as the curtain rises the „Mädchenklage" (XV. 1) sighs forth softly from the strains of the Öde. We are in the kingdom of the Grail and on the morning of that holy day Kundry's moans bring the grey headed Gurnemaz out of his hermitage.

I.

The finding of Kundry, the return of Parsifal, Kundry's baptism and blessing by the hero, with the closing episode of the

"Blumenaue", or the „Charfreitagszauber" devide the scene in the kingdom of the Grail into four parts. The scene is pervaded throughout by the spirit of Good Friday; as — on the morning of a holiday which rose shrouded in mist, the hope that the sun will break forth becomes a delightful certainty when the light rising gradually higher and higher shines out at last triumphant — so is it here; the Verödung, which predominates both in the accompaniements, and the songs, yields when nature arises purified, and Salvation proclaims in the glistening dewdrops of the Easter morning that the penitent sinner weeps.

Magic strains accompany the sighs of the returned wandrer, who remains invisible, and the Klingsor motive appears as though imagining that it still has power, "never thus did an animal grieve; but already at the words "sacred morning" a short charming melody (from the Entsühnungsgesang) (s. XXI. 1) which appears later on, breaks forth but is silenced by Kundry's deep sighs as her motive enters painfully, longingly, wresting itself free from the bonds of magic (s. XXI. 1. a.). — The quick movements of Gurnemanz as he goes towards the thorn hedge, from behind which the sighs issue forth, and tears the branches apart, are illustrated by a short instrumental movement, consisting of lively ascending figures, which passes into the Hingebungsmelodie (XIX) when the last concealing branch is torn away: "Ah — she once more here!" — And now with the last call of the old man to awake. — Winter has fled, spring is here" — there is for a short time a murmuring sound as though the joys of spring were breathing over us full of rapture and life: strains enter having the character of the "Entsühnungsmelodie". But again for one anxious moment, life ceases, when Gurnemanz finds Kundry lying "cold and stiff" as if dead; while he is busynig himself with her, a second, small, instrumental passage, musically illustrates his movements, and is introduced by a tender figure which seems to sigh longingly for the first Expiation melody (Page XXI. 1. *b*). But at every endeavour the sad voice of the "Verödung" is immediately heard through all the figurations of the accompaniment. At last, corresponding to the beginning of the scene, the "Mädchenklage" is heard in long drawn tones portraying the breathing of Kundry as she awakes from her deathlike sleep, and leads to a soft, zephyrlike rising of the Grail motive: — the Kundry motive starts up convulsively *ff*. — a shriek — consciousness returns — and she who was forever accursed awakes to Eternal spring and redemption.

XXI. 1. Die erste Ensühnungsmelodie.

a. (Kundry's tiefster Seufzer.)

b. (Sehnsuchtsseufzer n. d. Entsühnung.)

As she now arises and takes her first step in the domi nion of the Grail since we last saw her, that thematic succession of tones and chords which characterized her first appearance in the drama is again heard, but is now joined to a small triplet figure in the bass, which by soft trembling, expresses the astonishment of Gurnemanz at the change which has taken place in her. Now she is indeed Kundry the Helper — the server —, and her only words during the act — "to serve — to serve" — conclude with impressive simplicity this retrospection of the best moments of her former life.

She goes into the cottage to fetch the water pitcher for filling, and Gurnemanz astounded watches her as she goes — "how different now her gait!"

Gralmotiv.

We here encounter the charm of "Charfreitag" (Good Friday), whose motive from the "Liebesmahlspruch" (XVIII), thrills with holy awe, and bursting forth from the solemn Grailmotive it ends in the Elegiac close of the Holy Speech: — "oh! day of grace without compare" etc. — But this is not the end, from the dying away of the "Heilandswort" there is spun out tenderly and softly, but as if groping uncertainly, a lulling joybreathing melody full of gentle morning charm — the prophecy of the "Blumenaue": is fulfilled by the silent entrance of a new guest to the Grail, — one who comes with hesitating steps, as if in a trance — the Unexpected — the Seeker — Parsifal on his wanderings.

Parsifal's entrance is characterized by his own motive clothed in sad minor and, breaking off in strains of melancholy longing already often heard, it is borne down by the short faltering tones of the Öde motive, which sorrowfully succeeds, but does not so soon leave him. The ascending chromatic passage from the "Irren" of the introduction emerges several times in between. Gurnemanz now rebukes the sadly silent guest for bearing arms in the consecrated place on a holy day: his pious admonition is again accompanied, in strangely solemn harmony, by the Grail motive and the Charfreitagsmotive. — Thereupon Parsifal lays aside his arms and sinks upon his knees in mute prayer before the holy spear which he has stuck in the ground; Gurnemanz recognizes him — recognises the spear, and breaks at last from his awed astonishment into fervent thanksgiving Meanwhile Parsifal's prayer introduced by his own gloomy motive, to which the "Spear motive" is softly and slowly joined, is midway accompanied by the sacred strains of the "Liebesmahlspruch", enveloped in a solemn mystery of trembling, floating harmonies. Thereupon chromatically descending, there issues forth an intensely enthusiastic figure — "ah! which path did he find?": the Middle voice (hidden by the upper voice) of the Verheissungsspruch, whose Thoren motive is immediately heard, gives (with a slight touch of the Atonement melody") animation to the expressive echoing cres close of the Liebesmahlspruch, like the outpourings of a soul in a state of sublime rapture: "Oh! holiest day, to which I now awake!" With the "Heilands-klage" ending *ff*., and now appearing as a song of hope dispensing redeeming power, the Grail motive again enters "dim", as Parsifal rises and tenders his simple greeting to the "gray haired knight" — "happy I, again to have found thee!" — Most beautifully are these simple words joined to the corresponding refrain of the motive, but at Gurnemanz joyous reply the continuation of the „Öde motive", (from the beginning the Overture), theis followed by a small figure, which proves to be a rythmical shortening of that motive, and which later forms the chiet motive during Gurnemanz' narrative of the sufferings of the Grail knighthood (s. XX. 1.).

But before this narrative Parsifal addresses these present "by paths of doubt and suffering I came" — and these words, full of sorrow, self experienced, engrave on the soul the picture of his wanderings, already musically portrayed in the Overture. Thus we have here a repetition of the same motive figures. After the first measures of the syncopated "Irremotiv", the "Waldesmelodie" rushes in between and reminds us involuntarily of its affinity to the musical spirit of the "Atonement melody" of the "Blumenaue". Then at the passionate cry: — "to him, to whose deep lament I once in foolish wonder listened" — the "Leidensmotiv" of Amfortas (IV) breaks forth in the bass, and the "Thorenmotiv" follows in a some what longer phrase. At: — "alas! the way of salvation ne'er to find" — the "Irremotiv" again wanders and falters, (as in the Overture) till it reaches the despairing forebodings of the Grail motive — "when I thought I already knew him — then doubt seized me"; at the description of the fight over the holy relic, the second part of the Overture is repeated; the "Thorenmotiv" now boldly appears and gives fresh vigor to the musical movement, leading it to a final, triumphant outbreak of the now perfectly freed Grail motive "before thee gleams uninjured and sublime — the sacred spear of the Grail!"

The "Liebesmahlspruch" with an interlude of the

"Charfreitagsmotiv" immediately resounds at Gurnemanz' intensely joyful cry — "oh! grace, greatest salva ion!" —, and at the last words — "O holy, sublime wonder!" — when through the Elegiac close, delight finds vent in tears, the long silent "Glaubensthema" announces from on high the healing of all woe, and by a tender modulation leads to the beginning of Gurnemanz' narrative — "Ah! my lord, if t'was a curse — believe, it is removed". But with this modulation the "Glaubensthema" is changed into a melody which we have already heard at Gurnemanz' former cry of joy, as an upper voice to the "Thorenmotiv"; now singing with holy emotion of blessed purification and atonement it leads once more into the Grail motive — "here art thou, — this the dominion of the Gail." This picture of desolation and sorrow in the Grailurg causes a repetition of the beginning of the Overture; and the mention of the suffering, death-desiring Amfortas calls forth his „Wehelaute" with the Kundry motive. During the following part of the narration which portrays the general condition of the knighthood the shortened figure of the "Öde", before refered to, (XXI 1.) is led through many thematic changes

XX. 1. (Verkürztes Öde-Thema.)

Here a passage — „No more, a message comes to us" leads in a solemn, earnest manner, with the fundamental tones of the "Glockenthema", harmonically darkened, to the first warning of the mourning choruses, heard later at Titurel's obsequies; then it also dies away into the "Öde" motive — "In this corner of the forest I concealed myself" etc. Over the desolation of grief, now breathes, in lightest spiritlike *pp.*, a touching strain from the Titurel variation of the "Glaubensthema" (III. 2.) ending in the Grail motive — "Titurel my noble lord" — then, at the last repetition of the "Öde" motive stops, as if choking with emotion — "he died — a man — like all!"

A loud rcy of pain is wrung from Parsifal's breast — "and I — I am the cause of all this misery!" — Sorrowful longings for redemption pervade his song; the "Thorenmotiv" — "to bring deliverance I myself am chosen" — sinks as if fainting into silence: overcome by passionate pain Parsifal sinks senseless to the ground under the burden of sin for which he must atone. Kundry hastens to help him, brings water from the spring, bathes his forehead, loosens his coat of mail, and busies herself in tender, womanly acts — whereat the vehement upspringing movements of her "Stormy figure", subside and give place to a refrain of the "Hingebungsmelodie" (XIX) in two, short, gentle, long drawn out phrases which at the end sound as if pleading for salvation. Now all is silent — "Not so! — the holy spring itself shall make our pilgrim's bath refreshing." After a few, deep, sonorous tones of the "Glockemmotiv", the new theme of "Segen"-Blessing and "Taufe" Baptism (XXII) arises in solemn earnest harmony.

XXII. Der Segensspruch.

In the following part of the scene the new motive predominates, and appears four times, always as an introduction to the significant actions of feet washing, blessing, the anointment, of Parsifal and the baptism of Kundry. In a manner as gentle as solemn it unites the holy character of the Grail with that of tender Spring, which as living symbols of the Atonement and Resurrection surround these devout actions with an ever clearer meaning.

After the first "Segensspruch", the second "Entsühnungsmelodie", whose strains we have already noticed immediately follows, tenderly and joyously. It appears in two parts, and is heard both before and after the beautiful words of Gurnemanz — "And now shall the dust of his long pilgrimage be washed away" (XXI. ad. 2 + 2).

XXI. 2. Zweite und dritte Entsühnungsmelodie.

Already bright the morning sun shines down upon the dewy flowers, and into the redeemed souls of men; but the loud rejoicings of Deliverance and the delights of Easter are not allowable before the devout band of the faithful has been strengthened and glorified for the Last journey by the consecration of holy deeds of love. At these words — "the holy mount awaits us" — the solemn warning sounds of the "Trauerchor" (XXXIII) are heard, and they recall the condition of the knighthood when preparing for their last sorrowful feast. The motive of the "Verödung" again follows in its shortened form.

XXIII. Der Trauerchor.

Meanwhile Kundry begins her faithful task of feet washing; and as the eye of the reclining one turns upon her, an expressive repetition of that strain from her narrative in the second act — "I feel his eyes already on me" — accompanies the saving glance of the beloved hero, then ceases in tender loftiness and is tenderly resolved into the previous "Atonement melody" heard in the Overture (XXI. ad. 2.) "thou washest my feet let this friend and anoint my head." Gurnemanz words of sublime emotion — "blessed be thou, thou pure one, through purity" — are heard in the second

"Segensspruch" and as before the second "Atonement melody" (XXI. 2.) soars after it in soft dissolving brightness — "By thee all the sorrows of sin are softened!" — Accompanied by a light flowing figure, the "Segensspruch" is then repeated for the third time; it introduces the anointing of feet by Kundry, and like tender sighs expressing devout resignation and humble longing breathes through the music which softly accompanies this action, passing at last into the fervent strains of the "Mädchenklage" — "thou anointest my feet — let Titurel's comrade anoint my head" —, whereupon the "Parsifal motive" — "today as king he will greet me" — introduces *f.* the anointing of the head. The truly kingly greeting of Gurnemanz is joined with soulful fervor to this motive and to the connecting tones of its continuation — "thou pure, thou pitiful, patient one" —; and the "Thorenmotiv" with an accompanying figure, resembling the "Heilandsklage" flows into the Parsifal motive at the transition to the *ff* ascent of the Grail motive — "let the last weight be taken from his head." —

From this splendid majestic climax grand solemn chords lead to the fourth (*pp.*) appearance of the "Segensspruch" which now resounds as a holy, baptismal hymn — "thus I my first duty do perform" —; the Grail motive arises, and from it the "Glaubensthema" soars forth like the holy dove over the waters — "be baptised and believe in the Redeemer!" — At the baptism, this sacred theme falls blessingly on the head of the sinner, who is bending to the earth and weeping bitterly, then ceases in the expressive closing strain of the "Heilandsklage" (II Act: "then his gaze fell on me"); the look of the Saviour shines forgivingly from the eyes of His pure messenger on the weeping woman, now freed from her curse; — Redemption enters at the moment of the divine benediction as light penetrated into the world at the word of the Creator — from the last strains of the "Heilandsklage" the melodic web of the "Blumenaue" (XXIV) is softly spun out in gentle placid undulations.

The rich, pure magic of newly awakened spring is revealed, and loveliest voices singing of the joys of Redemption fill with softest rapture, the fragrant, blooming, dewy expanse of the beautiful, still world, on that sunny day of the Saviour. At Parsifal's tender cry of ecstasy — "ah! how beautiful seem the world today!" — the melody is worked out in canon form and is followed by the yearning, impulsive, and later gently soothing development of the first "Atonement melody" (XXI, 1.), which at the beginning of the act casts a gleam of hope over the desolation of the scene. But again it is silenced by gloomy strains — "that is the spell of Good Friday, my Lord" — whereat with an awful tremolo the "Liebesmahlsspruch" ascends to the "Charfreitagsmotiv", till with repeated sighs — "woe! saddest of days" — it is resolved in the conclusion of the speech — "thou see'st it is not so".

XXIV. Die Blumenaue.

A second time the "Blumenaue" emerges brilliantly from the the gloomy clouds of Good Friday and forms with its melody in canon form, a graceful sounding basis to Gurnemanz' instructive song upon the blessedness of Good Friday. An interlude of regular swaying movements from of the Grail motive — "in the Redeemer's loving foot steps, now every creature rejoices" — introduces a third appearance of the chief melody in triumphant *f*. — "Will their prayer hallow him?" etc. Once more, as a contrast, the vision of the Saviour on the Cross passes before us in heavy tritonic notes on the kettle drums — "she cannot see him upon the cross" —; and then, as if from intense longing to see the Saviour, the Close of the "Liebesmahlsspruch" arises with the Elegiac figure in an ascending sequence, until the previous "Entsühnungsmelodie" returns now fully develepod, and charmingly varied. — "now grasses and flowers appear in the meadows". A soft swelling chromatic passage — "as God with heavenly patience" — leads with softening dimuendo to the fourth entrance of the "Hauptmelodie"; again the wealth of melody rises to a soaring crescendo and at last the Grail motive rings through the "Blumenaue" resounding over all like the joyous, sacred, sublime triumph cry of Good — "Nature today pardoned regains her innocence". Thereupon a joyous variation of the "Entsühnungsmelodie" begins *f.* but gently subsides and ends, by means of the first Figuration of the melody, in the longing tones of the "Mädchenklage" — "I saw them perish who once mocked me." With the following words — "whether today they yearn for redemption?" — this passes softly into the "Heilandsklage" then gives place to the fifth, and last return of the principal melody of the "Blumenaue" in softest *pp.* The words of the song are tenderly interwoven with the melody and express sublimest joy — "thy tears too become blessed dew: thou weepest — see, the meadows rejoice."

Thereupon, like a sigh of blissful ecstasy, the refrain of the last Atonement melody wells up, but soon diminishes and again soars away: already we hear sounds of woe in these diminishing strains; distant bells, deprived of their former closing tones, give warning of the mournful celebration which is pending in the Grail mount, and the figure which constantly accompanies the succeeding "Panorama music", and the Funeral choruses (compare XXIII) is joined to their thematic tones. But over the oppressive solemnity of these strains the splendid Parsifal motive now rises triumphant, and accompanies the hero at the beginning of his journey to the sacred house of suffering. So we will accompany him with firm steps into the dark mysteries of the new transformation.

The Transformation Music.

Fearfully forbidding the Begleitungsfigure sounds through all the music as it rolls onward unceasingly; and therein are heard, falling like the grievous blows of Fate, the woeful strains of the fully developed Second motive of "Herzeleide" — a motive expressing indeed "Heart suffering" and the love sorrows of Mankind, and also every torment which Love imposed on the Redeemer himself! —

XVI. 2.

It is as though a picture of the life of our hero passed before us; from the sufferings of his mother's love till this journey of agony when he carries the cross of redemption: once more upon the last journey he must bear compassionately the whole weight of evil, that the world, to which he was called to bring salvation, with cruel severity laid upon him. — It is a sphere of deepest suffering upon which we enter with him, through which we advance as the motive leads us, horrible, yearning for deliverance, yet stubborn to every new blow of Fate; like Gurnemanz narrative it is wrapped in the harmonies of the "Verödung" and moves with painful deceptive cadences, each in succession follow the pitiless ever advancing steps of the Begleitungs figure, in which the sounds of the Bells intermingle, increasing they finally usher in a *ff*. development of the woeful lamenting Schluss-figure of the whole Interlude:

As the earlier Accompaniment (Begleitungs) figure, hitherto silent, advances anew and the "Ödemotiv" sounds now in full, the Grail-Temple is revealed to our gaze, and the knights clothed in gloomy funeral garments, some bearing Titurel's corpse, and others with Amfortas and the Grail, move from different sides amidst the antiphones of their double chorus.

II.

The bane of deep mourning and woeful despondency may yet be heard in the choruses of the knights, and the same musical means of expression are here made use of which we noticed in the Interlude of the previous scene at the mention of the celebration. They here form in a characteristic manner the melodic and harmonic formation of both choruses. It is worthy of notice that the first verses end four times in the Grail motive. The Sorrowful movement of the Interlude is joined to the choir which ac companies Amfortas, while the choir bearing Titurel's remains is accompanied by the Theme of the Bells. But as the alternate songs become shorter, the first figure from the "Verödung" brings the assembly to a pause with painful sounds of woe, and at the end as they all unite together in wild repetitions of that plaintive cry — "For the last time" — the struggling, pressing, Schluss-figure of the Interlude, derived from the melody at the beginning of the Overture, again enters and gives these cries an expression full of anguished lamentation. The Bells now ring out, and only cease at Amfortas' cry, faint with suffering — "Alas! alas! woe unto me" — thereupon the "Öde" motive is repeated in its abbreviated form.

The unveiling of Titurel's corpse calls forth *ff.* a piercing and rapid ascent of the "Leidensmotiv" (IV) which descends through three octaves, as if it fled at the sight of this supreme passion of pain, but it is immediately overcome by the soft sustained tones of a new motive sounding like a "Weihegruss" sacred greeting (XXV). Here the motive first forms a short "ritornel" to the prayer — "my father, most blessed of heroes" — before becoming the thematic foundation of the prayer itself, this is especially characteristic of all the greater songs of Amfortas. It breathes throughout with the noble repose of that proud, blissful time when Titurel reigned, At the words — "Oh! thou who now in splendor divine the Redeemer himself beholdest" —, it is resolved into the "Glaubensthema" and now one observes an inner, though not a authenticated relationship between these two themes.

XXV. Der Weihegruss für Titurel.

At this point the prayer refers to the revelation of the Grail and the "Liebesmahlsspruch" and the Grail motive again enter: but with the last sentence — "Death! death! the only mercy!" — a musical figure appears as a motive of Love's Woes in which a resemblance to the "Herzeleide" motive may be discerned; here it accompanies alone the last heartfelt, pleading words of Amfortas' prayer, first, with marvellous tenderness, and then in the form of a passionate lament.

XVI. 3. (Gebet des Amfortas.)

But the tumultuously rising importunate cries of the knights "Do thy duty! thou must! thou must!" — arouse anew in the wearied Amfortas feelings of the deepest despair. "No! no more!" — The "Leidensmotive" which accompanied him at the beginning of the drama now also at the end, when his soul rises in revolt against life, joins itself to him with wild passion in an extended, defiant, ascending form.

At the last words "Draw thy sword" the keenness of his despair is expressed, as at the corresponding portion of the Lament in the first act, by the devilish power of the Klingsor motive, now chasing before it rushing "magic movements" which at last dash into the Grail motive — "There the Grail itself shall give you light."

Parsifal — the new king of the Grail, has already entered with the healing weapon; as he advances, and a new and loftier realm is disclosed to view, the harmones of the Grail motive are marvellously altered — "only one weapon avails: only the spear which gave the wound can close it." — When with a touch of the spear he closes Amfortas' wound, all is transformed; the close of the Liebesmahlsspruch resounds, with the "Spear motive", joyously, proudly triumphant, and the Leidensmotive, which has just given expression to defiant, devilish passion now appears pacified and gentle, in the presence of suffering relieved (IV. 2.). "Blessed be thy suffering, which gave the timid Fool, Pity's greatest strength, and purest Wisdom's might." The "Thorenmotive" following the changed "Leidensmotiv", enters as a sublime symbol of pure triumph, swelling ever higher and higher, until the entrance of the triumphal song in the Parsifal motive, which with regal splendor accompanies Parsifal as he advances to the middle of the stage — "The holy Spear! — I bring it back to you!" Then the "Liebesmahlsspruch" and the Glaubensthema (Form III 3.) greet with a short solemn song this reunion of the Grail and the Spear; the Liebesmahlsspruch taking no longer the "Pain Figure", in which it formerly bewailed the sacred wound of suffering, soars unfettered to blessed freedom (I. 3.) and retains to the close of the act this new form, which portrays the power of God's love as revealed by the Word of Redemption.

I. 3. (Liebesmahlspruch als Erlösungswort.)

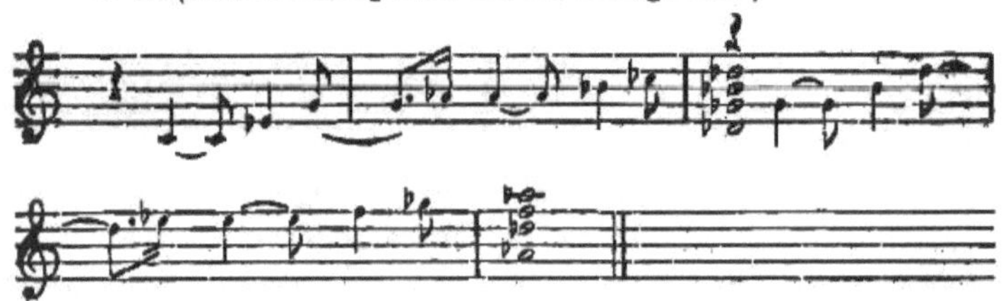

"Oh! wonders of joy sublime" — this last sacred, rapturous song of the new king begins with the "Glaubensthema" — and here, as at the end of the Overture the ascending "Spear motive", with the "Elegiac Figure" and the "Heilands-klage" itself express the healing of sorrow and its change to soul blessedness. The "Thorenmotive" and the "Erlösungs-wort" form a refrain, as Parsifal mounts the steps of the scantuary giving in his Last words his first Kingly command "Reveal the Grail! — Open the shrine" Amid strains as of golden harps the Grail motive announces the unveiling of the long-concealed blessing-giver, and at Parsifal's silent prayer it is followed by the holy, closely related "Erlösungswort" and "Glaubensthema", one the celestical flower of the other's divine love cravings. A divine glory streams from on high through the deep shades of the hall; at the words "highest holy miracle" — the choirs softly begin with the "Thoren" motive which here appears manifested as a real "Heilandsmotiv"; and at the words — "Redemption to the Redeemer" — the "Erlösungsworte" rising from the deep voices of the men passes through the choir of youths and ascends to the boys, who bear it above all the other voices to the highest height, and there, on long held tones, like the Sun of Eternity it sends forth beams of glorious divine light. The Glaubensthema sinks down from the heights with softest flutterings while the voices intermingle like spirits of light joyously playing together in a state of blessed unity; the Holy Dove soars as if in blessing over Parsifal's head, white he gently swings the Grail before the upturned gaze of the knights; Kundry sinks to the ground, her spirit passing away amidst the sacred strains; and as now the Grail motive in all its solemn splendor comes forward to render homage to the new King it seems to disclose once more newer, higher, and purer spheres of divine wonder, through which the "Glaubensthema" joyously flows like a shimmering river of light. So the visible reality of this sublime scene, fading from sight, is enveloped in a heavenly ether of more than earthly happiness, through which fulltoned to the end, the divine "Erlösungswort", from the last Grail motive, soars released to realms of bliss eternal.

Steinway & Sons
New York.
London. Hamburg.
European Branch Factory
Steinway's Pianofabrik
St. Pauli, Neue Rosenstrasse 20—24
Hamburg, (Germany).

Verlag von Georg Esseger in Leipzig.

Allen Besuchern

von

Richard Wagners Dramen

sind unentbehrlich

die Führer (Thematische Leitfaden) durch Dichtung und Musik

von

A. Jahn, Ferd. Pfohl und H. von Wolzogen

Bd.		brosch.	geb.
I.	Jahn, ***Flieg. Holländer*** (nur Dichtung) . .	M. 0.20	—
II.	„ ***Lohengrin***, 2. Auflage (Dicht. u. Musik)	„ 1.—	1.50
III.	Pfohl, ***Meistersinger***, 4. Aufl. „ „ „	„ 1.—	1.50
IV.	„ ***Tannhäuser***, 4. Aufl. „ „ „	„ 1.—	1.50
V.	v. Wolzogen, ***Ring***. 150.—160. T. „ „ „	„ 1.—	1.50
VI.	„ ***Tristan u. Isolde***, 16. Aufl. „ „ „	„ —.75	1.25
VII.	„ ***Parsifal***, 22. Aufl. „ „ „	„ 2.—	2.50

In englischer Sprache ist bisher erschienen:

Guide trough the music of Richard Wagners

		brosch.	geb.
Ring of the Nibelung (v. Wolzogen)	3. ed. . . .	M. 2.—	2.50
Tristan and Isolde „	3. „	„ 1.—	1.50
Parsifal (v. Wolzogen)	3. „	„ 2.—	2.50

In französischer Sprache:

L'Anneau du Nibelung (3. éd.) Guide musical . 1.50 2.—

Man achte genau auf die Namen der Verfasser und des Verlegers, da viele minderwertige Nachahmungen erschienen sind.

Ferner sei empfohlen:

The New Opera Glass:

Containing the plots of the most popular operas and a short biography of the composers. By **Fr. Charley.** 4. verb. u. verm. Auflage. 190 Seiten 8⁰, holzfreies Papier. Elegant Ganzleinen flexibel geb. M. 2.—.

Verlag von Georg Esseger in Leipzig.

Erläuterungen zu Richard Wagners Nibelungen-Drama

von **Hans von Wolzogen.** 14. Auflage. Preis M. 1.—.

Inhalt: I. Das Bayreuther Nationaltheater. — Wagners nationale Idee. — Bayreuth — ein Bedürfnis der deutschen Kunst. — Der Ort des Nationaltheaters. — Die Wirkungen der Festspiele. — II. Das Nibelungen-Drama. — Wagners Schlussworte nach dem ersten Cyklus. — Das Scenische: kritiko- und zoologische Bedenklichkeiten. — Die Musik: Längen und Leitmotive. — Die poetische Form. Stabreim und Sprache. — Die Dichtung: ethische Grundidee, poetische Behandlung des Sagenstoffes, nationale Bedeutung.

Erläuterungen

zu Max Bruch's Komposition **„Das Lied von der Glocke"** (Gedicht von Schiller). Mit vielen Notenbeispielen von Aug. Jahn. 24 Seiten 8°. Eleg. brosch. M. —.40.

Die „Deutsche Musikerzeitung" schreibt: . . . Zahlreiche Notenbeispiele helfen das Verständnis vermitteln, so dass es sich sehr erfolgreich erweisen würde, wenn überall, wo das Werk zur Aufführung kommt, dies Heftchen statt eines sonst üblichen Textbuches, das ja von Schillers Glocke überflüssig ist, den Zuhörern in die Hand gegeben würde.

Richard Wagner und Schopenhauer.

Eine Darlegung der philosophischen Anschauungen Richard Wagners an der Hand seiner Werke von Dr. **Fr. von Hausegger.** 2. vermehrte und verbesserte Auflage. Eleg. brosch. M. 1.—.

Denksteine aus dem Leben berühmter Tonkünstler.

Auf Grund charakteristischer Dokumente veröffentlicht von Prof. Dr. **Ludwig Nohl.** 530 Seiten gr. 8°. 2. Auflage. Preis hochelegant gebunden M. 7.—.

Der unermüdlich thätige, um die Sammlung, Sichtung und Erläuterung der musikalischen Produktivität und graphischer Daten so verdiente einstige Heidelberger Professor Dr. Ludwig Nohl, giebt in diesem hochinteressanten Werke eine Reihe von Studien, reich an mannigfacher Anregung, durchwoben mit vielfachen, bisher noch völlig unbekannten Notizen über das Leben und Wirken, sowie aus dem handschriftlichen Nachlasse der hervorragendsten deutschen Tonkünstler. — Dieses hochelegant ausgestattete Buch empfiehlt sich auch als herrliches Gelegenheitsgeschenk für jeden Musikalisch-Gebildeten.

Die Aussicht der Kunst Richard Wagners in Frankreich.

Von Dr. **P. Marsop.** Zweite Auflage. 8°. Broschiert Mark 1.—.

Geistvoll und sehr überzeugend. (Illustr. Deutsche Monatsschrift.)

Was ist Styl? Was will Wagner? Was soll Bayreuth?

Betrachtungen über die Idee einer Stylbildungsschule in Bayreuth von **Hans von Wolzogen.** 3. Ausgabe. Preis geheftet M. 1.—.

Verlag von Georg Esseger in Leipzig.

Die Bühnenfestspiele in Bayreuth, ihre Gegner und ihre Zukunft, von **M. Plüddemann.** 4 Bogen gr. 8°. Preis gebunden M. —.60.

Richard Wagners Frauengestalten [Brünnhilde — Kundry] von **Cl. Freiherr von Schwerin.** Broschiert M. 1.50.

Poetische Laut-Symbolik. Psychische Wirkungen der Sprachlaute im Stabreime aus Richard Wagners „Ring des Nibelungen", versuchsweise bestimmt von **Hans von Wolzogen.** 3. Auflage. 3 1/2 Bogen 8°. Preis geheftet M. 1.—.

Die Sprache in Richard Wagners Dichtungen. Von **Hans von Wolzogen.** Inhalt: I. Zur künstlerischen Stilistik. II. Zur grammatischen Stilistik. III. Zur Wortbildung und zum Wortgebrauch. 2. Auflage. 9 Bogen. gr. 8°. Preis broschiert M. 1.25.

1849 Der Aufstand in Dresden. Ein geschichtlicher Rückblick zur Rechtfertigung Richard Wagners von **William Ashton Ellis.** Deutsche Ausgabe in Übereinstimmung mit dem Verfasser redigiert von Hans von Wolzogen. Preis broschiert M. 1.—.

Richard Wagner-Porträt in Stahlstich. Gestochen von dem rühmlichst bekannten Künstler **A. Weger** sen. Preis pro Blatt auf Kupferdruckpapier, Format 28×39 cm, M. 1.—; Chines. Papier, Format 28×39 cm, M. 2.—.

Ein herrlicher Zimmerschmuck.

Verlag von Georg Esseger in Leipzig.

Die reform. Weltanschauung in Richard Wagners letzten Werken. **Emil Barden.** 135 Seiten 8° broschiert M. 1.—.

Freyhoff, Bayreuth 1913. (Ein Mahnruf an die deutsche Nation.) M. —.50.

Richard Wagner in seinem Hauptwerk Der Ring des Nibelungen. Von **Karl Gjellerup.** Mit Autorisation des Verfassers übersetzt von Dr. **Otto Luitpold Jiriczek.** 3., vom Verfasser eigens durchgesehene und dem dänischen Original gegenüber vermehrte und verbesserte Ausgabe. 15 Bogen broschiert M. 3.—, gebunden M. 4.—.

Hamburger Nachrichten: . . . Dieses Werk ist unbedingt das hervorragendste auf dem vielbeackerten Felde der Richard-Wagner-Literatur. . . .

Die Vossische Zeitung sagt u. a.: Das so anspruchslos auftretende Büchlein kann allen, welche einer Einführung in Wagners Trilogie zu bedürfen glauben, nicht warm genug empfohlen werden. Der Verfasser erzählt jedes der vier Einzeldramen erst in Kürze seinem Inhalte nach, immer unter Hinweis auf die hauptsächlichsten Leitmotive, und betrachtet es dann in seinem Verhältnis zu dem von Wagner vorgefundenem Stoff und seinen Quellen.

Zur Verständigung. Ein Beitrag zur Wagner-Sache von Prof. **C. R. Hennig** in Posen. Preis broschiert M. 1.—.

Die Musik und ihre Klassiker in Aussprüchen Richard Wagners. 2. Auflage. Preis broschiert M. 1.50.

Die vorliegende Sammlung von Aussprüchen Richard Wagners soll erstens den Freunden des Meisters die altgewohnten und vertrauten Stellen in einer übersichtlichen Folge vor Augen führen, damit sie ihnen nach Bedürfnis leichter gegenwärtig seien, und zweitens einen Beitrag zur Ausbreitung des Verständnisses Wagners bei der großen Masse derer abgeben, die ihm besonders fremd und gleichgültig gegenüberstanden. Die Auswahl ist ihrem Zwecke gemäß mit Umsicht und Geschmack getroffen und bietet geistvolle und bildende Unterhaltungslektüre für Laien und Eingeweihte.

Verlag von Georg Esseger in Leipzig.

Alle Eltern und Erzieher, die ihren Kindern oder Pflegebefohlenen Klavier-Unterricht erteilen lassen wollen, haben im eigenen Interesse die Pflicht, sowohl auf gute Lehrer, wie letztere wiederum auf gute Unterrichtsmittel, auf praktische und zweckmäßige Klavierlehrbücher bedacht zu sein. Je einfacher, praktischer und faßlicher die Unterrichtsmethode ist, um so größer werden naturgemäß auch die Erfolge und Fortschritte sein.

Den bisher im Gebrauche befindlichen Klavierschulen reiht sich nunmehr eine weitere an, die unter dem Titel

Klaviermethode der Elementarstufe

von **Karl Heuser**

in meinem Verlage erschienen ist.

Der Verfasser ist ein allerfahrener und bewährter **Klavier-Pädagoge.** Mehr als 30 Jahre hat er sein System in seinem Unterrichts-Institut erprobt und praktisch zur Anwendung gebracht, und zwar mit einem Erfolge, der ihm das unumschränkteste Lob auch der tüchtigsten Musikverständigen eingebracht hat.

Die hervorstechenden Vorteile dieser neuen Klavierschule sind:

Einfachheit in der Methode,
Praktisch in der Anwendung
und Systematisch im Aufbau.

Ein Fachmann urteilte dahingehend, daß

Heusers Klavierschule ihren Weg in die deutsche Familie in gewaltigem Zuge machen wird.

Diese neue, epochemachende Klavierschule, deren Preis trotz der durchaus soliden Ausstattung **nur 2 Mark 50 Pfg.** beträgt, sei hiermit allen Musiklehrern angelegentlichst empfohlen.

Ebenso:

Wie spiele ich am besten Klavier?

Eine Methodik des Klavierunterrichts von KARL HEUSER.

4 Bg. 8°. Elegant brosch. Mk. —.60

„— — Heuser ist ein Klavierpädagoge, wie sie alle sein müßten, aber deren leider zu wenige gibt. Seine Worte sind Goldkörner der Wahrheit" usw.
(Deutsche M.-Musikerztg.)

„— — Ein sehr verdienstliches kleines Büchlein, das alle Eltern lesen sollten, die es ernst mit der musikalischen Erziehung ihrer Kinder usw. nehmen — —."
(St. Galler Bl).

Verlag von Georg Esseger in Leipzig.

Von den Hoh. Behörden angelegentlichst z. Anschaffung empfohlen:

Gesetzeskunde und Volkswirtschaftslehre

I. Teil: Pache-Walther, **Die Lehre vom Staate,** 3., vermehrte und verbesserte Auflage. Preis brosch. M. 1.50, geb. M. 2.25.

II. Teil: O. Pache, **Die Lehre von der Gesellschaft,** Volkswirtschaftslehre. 3. Auflage. Preis brosch. M. 3.—, geb. M. 4.—.

In knappster Form, aber in erschöpfender und leichtverständlicher Weise machen uns diese beiden Bücher mit dem gesamten Staatsbetrieb — der Gesetzgebung und Gesetzausführung durch die betreffenden Behörden, den Rechten und Pflichten der Bürger — sowie der Geschichte der Nationalökonomie und der Wirtschaftspolitik bekannt. Sie sollten jedem Staatsbürger bekannt sein.

Buchführung und Wechsellehre

von Dr. M. Hardtmann. 4. Aufl. Preis M. 1.50.

Die rechtliche Natur des Schecks.

Inaugural-Dissertation von Ref. Kurt Heise. Preis M. 1.—.

Inhalt: Geschichte und wirtschaftliche Bedeutung des Schecks. Der Begriff des Schecks. Die Rechtsverhältnisse bei dem Scheck. Besondere Arten von Schecks.

Deutsches Recht.

Gesamtausgabe der am 1. Januar 1900 in Kraft getretenen Reichsgesetze und Verordnungen nebst den Preußischen Ausführungsgesetzen, Verordnungen und Verfügungen, bearbeitet und herausgegeben von Otto von Hentig, Herzogl. Sächs. Staatsminister, in Verbindung mit F. Siber, Regierungsrat, R. Chrzescinki, Regierungsrat a. D., K. Klee, Dr. jur. Über 1000 S. Text. Ladenpreis: Geb. in Orig.-Hlbfrbd. mit Metallecken M. 15.—.

Die 29 Gesetze und 11 Bekanntmachungen und Verfügungen sind alle einheitlich organisch bearbeitet; es ist immer auf parallele und erläuternde Paragraphen anderer Gesetze hingewiesen.

Die „Magdeburgische Zeitung" schreibt u. a.: ... Große Arbeit erscheint dadurch in bescheidenster Form vor uns. Dem Ganzen ist ein mit außerordentlicher Sorgfalt bearbeitetes Sachregister von 84 Seiten Umfang beigegeben. Der Druck ist klar u. übersichtlich, die Zusammenstellung in einem stattlichen Band für den praktischen Gebrauch sehr wertvoll u. der Preis äußerst mäßig.

„Das Recht", Rundschau für den deutschen Juristenstand: Die umfassenden und einschneidenden Veränderungen, welche das Jahr 1900 uns auf fast allen Gebieten des Rechts gebracht hat, haben wohl in jedem Juristen den Wunsch erstehen lassen, eine zuverlässige, umfaßende und nicht zu teure Ausgabe der am 1. Januar 1901 in Geltung sich befindenden Reichsgesetze in einem handlichen Bande zu besitzen. Die obengenannte Ausgabe besitzt alle diese Vorzüge in hohem Grade, ja sie enthält für sämtliche Käufer noch den Vorzug, daß sie bei den einzelnen Paragraphen Verweisungen auf einschlägige andere Gesetzesstellen bringt und dadurch den inneren Zusammenhang der einzelnen Gesetze dem Auge bloßlegt und darauf aufmerksam macht; für die preußischen Käufer bietet sie außerdem den weiteren Vorteil, daß sie auch die preußischen Ausführungsgesetze, Verordnungen und Verfügungen zum Ausdruck bringt. Wir sind überzeugt, daß die handliche und sehr gut ausgestattete Ausgabe besonders für den preußischen Juristen von großem Wert ist.

Verlag von Georg Esseger in Leipzig.

Aktionär u. Gläubiger i. Konkurs d. Aktiengesellsch. Eine Abhandl. üb. Reservefonds u. Regreßanspruch v. Rechtsanw. **H. Burckas I.** Ca. 5 Bg. gr. 8°, eleg. brosch. M. 1.50.

Der Aufsichtsrat der Aktiengesellschaft, seine Rechte und Pflichten. Von Dr. jur. **Küntzel.** Preis brosch. M. 2.—.

Der Zusammenbruch so mancher Aktiengesellsch. hat in neuerer Zeit das allgemeine Interesse auf den Aufsichtsrat gelenkt. Vielfach wurde er für das hereinbrechende Unglück verantwortlich gemacht.

Der Herr Verfasser hat an der Hand der gesamten einschlägigen Literatur in überaus klarer Weise die Rechte und Pflichten des Aufsichtsrats und seiner Mitglieder genau festgestellt und praktische Winke erteilt, i. welch. Weise manch. Unheil vermieden werden kann.

Ist auch das vorliegende Werkchen in erster Linie für den Juristenstand geschrieben, so ist doch die Sprache so allgemein verständlich, daß auch die vielen Mitglieder der Aufsichtsräte von Aktiengesellschaften (aber auch der Gesellschaften mit beschränkter Haftung und der eingetragenen Genossenschaften) sich mit Nutzen in das Studium des Buches vertiefen werden. Ihnen muß doch vor allen daran liegen, ein genaues objektives Bild ihrer Rechte und Pflichten zu haben und in Zweifelsfällen einen zuverlässigen Berater in dem Werkchen zu finden.

Endlich aber kann auch dem großen Publikum, welches sich kapitalistisch an gewerblichen Großbetrieben beteiligt, die Lektüre dieser Schrift nicht angelegentlich genug empfohlen werden.

Das fiduziarische Indossament. Von Dr. jur. **Julius Steinblinck.** Preis broschiert M. 1.—.

Die deutsche Wechselordnung kennt bekanntlich das Voll-Indossament und das Prokura-Indossament. Oft indossiert man den Wechsel durch Vollindossament mit der Nebenverabredung, das Indossament nur im Rahmen eines Prokura-Indossaments zu gebrauchen, sog. fiduziarische Indossament.

Der in Theorie und Praxis entstandene lebhafte Streit, welche rechtliche Stellung einem fiduziarischen Indossatar zukommt, hat durch den Herrn Verfasser eine sehr gewandte und gründliche Darlegung und Prüfung gefunden. Insbesondere sind die praktisch so bedeutsamen Folgen eines fiduziarischen Indossaments sorgfältig erörtert und festgestellt.

Zu diesem Zwecke hat sich der Herr Verfasser im Eingang über Wesen und Wirkungen des Indossaments überhaupt ausgesprochen und die überaus streitige Frage untersucht, welche Einreden dem Voll-Indossator entgegengesetzt werden können.

Die Anschaffung des Werkchens wird deshalb nicht nur dem Richter, Rechtsanwalt u. Rechtslehrer, sondern vornehmlich der Geschäftswelt u. allen, d. mit Wechseln zu tun haben, sehr empfohlen.

Verlag von Georg Esseger in Leipzig.

Zur Theorie des Schönen.

Neue Formulierungen

von

Robert Mayrhofer-Brixen.

I. Grundprinzipien. ....

II. Die Künste und ihre Verbindung. ....

III. Schlußfolgerungen für die moderne Musik (R. Strauß).

Preis broschiert M. 1.—.

Der Verfasser des Aufsehen erregenden Werkes „Der Kunstklang“ gibt in der kleinen, inhaltsvollen Schrift **„Zur Theorie des Schönen“** eine kurzgefaßte, aber tief eindringende Darlegung der Prinzipien einer neuen Ästhetik, wie sie durch die bedeutendsten Erscheinungen insbesondere auf dem Gebiete der neueren Musik geradezu notwendig geworden ist; u. a. wird der schon von Wagner beanstandete schiefe Begriff des „Gesamtkunstwerkes“ richtig gestellt, sowie die jüngste Wendung der dramatischen Musik, am Beispiele der „Elektra“ von R. Strauß, streng objektiv beurteilt und ästhetisch eingeordnet.

Parsifal.

Die Religionskraft der Zukunft

von

E. Hellmut.

Preis geb. M. 2.50. Luxusausgabe geb. M. 5.—.

„Das Buch wendet sich an das intuitive Empfinden der Seele und hat den Zweck, die aus uralter Weisheit aufgebaute geniale Neuschöpfung Wagners dem Neuling verständlich zu machen und diejenigen zur Tat anzuregen und zu leiten, die den Weg eines zu innerer Harmonie führenden Lebens gehen wollen.“

☛ Durch alle **Buchhandlungen** des In- und Auslandes oder direkt gegen Einsendung des Betrages in Briefmarken vom Verlage **Georg Esseger in Leipzig** zu beziehen.

Guide

through the music, legend and poem of

Rich. Wagner

"The Ring of the Nibelun

(Der Ring des Nibelungen)

Price: 2 sh 6 d (M 2.50) bound, unbound 2 sh (M 2.—)

3. edition

Rich. Wagner "Parsifal"

Price: 2 sh 6 d (M 2.50) bound, unbound 2 sh (M 2.)

3. edition

R. Wagner "Tristan and Isold

Price: 1 sh (M 1.—) unbound.

by **Hans von Wolzogen** translated by
Ernst von Wolzogen

The New Opera Glass

Containing the plots of the most popular ope
and a short biography of the composers.

By

Fr. Charley.

4. edition, revised and augmented.

Price: 2 sh (M 2.—) bound.

GEORG ESSEGER, PUBLISHER, LEIPZ

Zeitfracht Medien GmbH
Ferdinand-Jühlke-Straße 7
99095 Erfurt, Deutschland
produktsicherheit@kolibri360.de